BIRDS

OF

OTTAWA

AND VICINITY

GERALD McKEATING
Illustrated by EWA PLUCIENNIK

LONE
PINE

Any request for photocopying, recording, taping or information storage and retrieval systems of any part of this book shall be directed in writing to the Canadian Reprography Collective, 379 Adelaide Street West, Suite M1, Toronto, Ontario M5V 1S5.

The Publisher:
Lone Pine Publishing
#206 10426-81 Avenue
Edmonton, Alberta, Canada
T6E 1X5

Canadian Cataloguing in Publication Data
McKeating, Gerald.
    Birds of Ottawa

Includes bibliographical references.

ISBN 0-919433-64-2

1. Birds - Ontario - Ottawa. 2. Bird watching
- Ontario - Ottawa. I. Pluciennik, Ewa, 1954-
II. Title.
QL685.5.O5M235 1990 598.29713'84 C90-091040-2

Cover Design: Ewa Pluciennik
Colour Illustrations: Ewa Pluciennik, Kitty Ho
Black and White Illustrations: Donna McKinnon, Ewa Pluciennik
Book Design and Layout: Yuet Chan, Michael Hawkins, Beata Kurpinski
Editorial: Jane Spolding, Mary Walters Riskin, Phillip Kennedy
Printing: Kyodo Printing Co. (S'pore) Pte. Ltd., Singapore

Publisher's Acknowledgement
The publisher gratefully acknowledges the assistance of the Federal Department of Communications, Alberta Culture and Multiculturalism, the Canada Council, and the Alberta Foundation for the Literary Arts in the production of this book.

CONTENTS

PREFACE

Most of us have some interest in nature and have been intrigued at one time or another by birds. An unusual duck on the river, a flash of red in the garden, loons at the cottage or the cheerful chickadee at the feeder: these moments have brought us enjoyment, and perhaps awakened a greater interest in our surroundings. Many people enjoy feeding birds and like to have them around the garden or cottage. This appreciation of birds gives us some contact with nature, no matter how slight, in an environment increasingly consumed by urban life.

This book is for people who are not necessarily active bird-watchers, but who just want to know a little bit more about the common species around them. There are many excellent bird books more comprehensive than this: this book is for the casual garden observer and it is hoped that it will provide a stimulus to dig deeper into the fascinating world of birds.

Each bird in this book is illustrated in colour with a brief description of some of the characteristics of the species. An overview of the urban habitats is provided as well as some ideas on attracting birds to your property. The sequence of species accounts follows the family order as presented by W. Earl Godfrey, *Birds of Canada*, revised edition, 1986.

For many years, Ontario has had the benefit of the efforts from many naturalists clubs and dedicated volunteers in the conserving of natural areas and the heightening of the awareness of nature. Public interest in nature has never been greater than it is today, and it is due in part to the efforts of these involved volunteers. To them, this book is dedicated.

ACKNOWLEDGEMENTS

Many thanks to Bruce M. DiLabio of the Canadian Nature Federation and to Loney Dickson, for their helpful comments on the manuscript, and to Ewa Pluciennik for her paintings.

Thanks to my wife and fellow birdwatcher, Patricia Crossley, who typed in the manuscript.

I would also like to express my gratitude to the Federation of Ontario Naturalists (FON) for letting us include their helpful *Checklist of Ontario Birds*. The FON is a non-profit wildlife organization with seventy-seven affiliated environmental and natural history groups. The FON's quarterly magazine, *Seasons*, regularly publishes a column on bird behaviour and identification, called "Birder's Notebook." In addition to the *Checklist*, the FON has also published a series of bird recordings, a children's book entitled *Birdwise*, and the *Atlas of Breeding Birds of Ontario*.

Most of all, I would like to recognize the extraordinary contribution of the many naturalists throughout the Ottawa region who have given so much of their time to interest others in the wonderful world of birds.

BIRDS IN THE CITY

FOR ANYONE with an interest in the environment, birds provide a very real and tangible way of identifying with nature. Whether on a busy downtown city street or in a remote part of a national park, birds surround us and are comparatively easy to see and to appreciate — without the need for special knowledge or equipment. Over the last decade more and more people have taken up birdwatching in their spare time and today it is the fastest growing recreational activity in the western world. Whether one actually goes out on a hike to look for birds, or merely appreciates them as part of another recreational activity, birdwatching greatly enhances one's enjoyment of the outdoors.

Many of us live in cities, but this in no way diminishes the possibilities or the pleasures in looking for birds. Birds, like people, have adapted to the urban situation, and their variety and abundance in the city can be a constant source of fascination to anyone who cares to look. Many of the habitats in urban areas resemble natural habitats, while others are strictly urban and attract their own fauna. Some of the more aggressive and common species, including Rock Doves (pigeons), European Starlings, House Sparrows, and Ring-billed Gulls, have adapted to man's environment, with its structures and its garbage.

The back yard is a good place for birdwatching. Even the newest subdivisions will have their bird "pioneers" although the variety of species at first will be small. Older residential neighbourhoods will have many more species because of the greater number and types of trees and bushes.

Back yards are by no means the only place in the city to see birds. In parks and open spaces, it is possible to see flycatchers, warblers, hawks and owls. Ottawa occupies a favorable location on the river which is bisected by the Rideau system as well. The natural areas and parks are just waiting to be explored.

Many birds can also be seen in the core. The obvious species such as Rock Doves and House Sparrows are well known, but I have seen thrushes and White-throated Sparrows scratching for food in the bushes along the canal, and I have observed Common Loons from the pavilion at Dows Lake. Thanks to recent introduction programs, even Peregrine Falcons can sometimes be seen. On warm summer nights, we can easily hear Common Nighthawks as they "hawk" for the insects attracted to the city lights.

To fully appreciate the diverse birdlife in the region, explore various habitats. Try Shirleys Bay along the Ottawa River and the wetlands at Britannia or Mer Bleue. The woodlands in the Gatineau are a common place to bird watch, yet the trees in Vincent Massey Park can also be alive with birds. Don't forget your own residential neighbourhood. By visiting different habitats, your appreciation and enjoyment of birds will grow with each trip.

HABITATS

The "habitat" of a bird is a place which provides all the basic necessities of life for that bird at some point. The term embraces the diversity of vegetation, nesting cover, food supply, escape routes, water, soils and climate. A habitat has the elements necessary for life. Each bird species has specific needs, and lives in the habitat best suited to its needs.

Wetlands

Wetlands are highly attractive to many species of birds. The habitats are varied from bog areas like Mer Bleue, to beaver-created wooded swamps or cattail marshes associated with the river. Even artificial wetlands like the sewage lagoons at Munster can provide excellent birdwatching opportunities.

Some wetlands are very temporary in nature. Examples are the flooded agricultural areas east of Bourget, near Riceville. During the spring, migrants like Canada Geese and Northern Pintails gather here by the thousands, feeding on left-over corn from the harvest. The shallow water warms quickly, creating an abundance of invertebrate life: a vital source of protein for the hens who will soon commence egg laying.

The marshlands along the Ottawa River can accommodate ducks, geese, herons, blackbirds and rails. In areas of poor agricultural land, where wet areas abound, the Common Snipe is a familia species. Lower Duck Island is a particularly good area, as are the marshes on the north side of the river. Mud Lake at Britannia is another place that should be explored. Watch for Wood Ducks, American Black Ducks, and herons here.

The Ottawa River

In addition to the marshes associated with the river, the river itself provides habitat for a variety of species. As well, it serves as a migration corridor for species who reside much further north. Careful observation at the right time of year could yield sightings of Brant, Arctic Tern or Red-throated Loon.

Common Goldeneye and Common Merganser can be seen easily in the winter on areas of fast-flowing open water, such as the stretches of the river overlooked by Bate Island at the Champlain Bridge, or by Deschênes.

Deschênes Rapids is a good birdwatching spot year-round. Gulls and Double-crested Cormorants can be seen and diving ducks are often on the river. Further west from Britannia to Andrew Haydon Park, large mud flats can be exposed in the fall. Here, shorebirds are common as well as gulls, ducks and geese.

Shirleys Bay is yet another habitat associated with the river. Reputed to be the best birdwatching spot in Ottawa, it provides a diversity of habitat including dryland forest, flooded maple swamp, marsh and the river itself. Quiet back-bay areas are popular with migrant birds, for feeding or loafing. There is a large causeway that extends well out into the river, which provides excellent viewing opportunities.

Open Space

Throughout the Capital region, every open space provides a habitat for birds. Trees and shrubs can be found in cemeteries, neighbourhoods and parks such as Vincent Massey, Rockcliffe, or the Arboretum, which offer abundant berries and seeds. In these areas, the vegetation is varied in density and height, providing habitats for birds that live in the treetops as well as those which inhabit the lower shrub layer. Ample cover is available for nesting.

Hydro transmission rights-of-way provide the right conditions for field birds like Eastern Meadowlarks, Savannah Sparrows or

Eastern Kingbirds. The broad roadsides of our parkways can provide similar habitat. In addition, these routes can serve as corridors between different habitats, a linkage that adds to bird species' diversity and survival.

Gardens and back lanes can offer habitat for some of the more common species, but industrial land often has the right conditions for more unusual species. The large quarry near Woodward Avenue has, on more than one occasion, been the winter home for a Gyrfalcon. Some of the larger industrial complexes are areas of regenerating habitat. Parts of these areas are undisturbed and gradually plant succession begins to restore the area to natural conditions. Small mammals thrive, and in winter, birds of prey can survive on the food provided by mice.

The agricultural land or weedy fields outside the city provide conditions for many open country species. Wintering hawks and owls hunt for mice, Snow Buntings feed on the weed seeds and Horned Larks gather seeds in late winter. In summer, American Goldfinches, Field Sparrows, Mourning Doves and many others can be found. Gray Partridges are often found south of the airport although the agricultural fields and manure piles of the central Experimental Farm can be more reliable.

Woodlands

There are many interesting woodlands in our region and fortunately, the National Capital Commission has much of it under its jurisdiction. Additional lands are owned by the municipality, the conservation authority or the Ministry of Natural Resources.

Our woodlands contain sugar maple, yellow birch, eastern hemlock, white birch, white pine and a carpet of spring wildflowers and ferns. The fall colour of our upland forest is so colourful as to be beyond the imagination — it is a beautiful time to watch for birds in these areas. Typical birds of this habitat type include Rose-breasted Grosbeak, Eastern Wood Pewee and Red-eyed Vireo.

There are many places to choose from within the Greenbelt area but for me, Gatineau Park, with its vast array of trees, is hard to beat. The Mackenzie King Estate, Old Chelsea Ravine, or the forests north of the Champlain Lookout are among the best of many fine areas. Closer to home, Mud Lake at Britannia is very good.

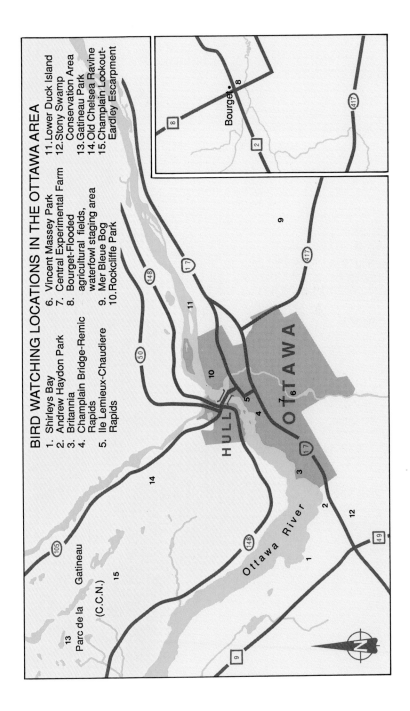

BIRD WATCHING LOCATIONS IN THE OTTAWA AREA

1. Shirleys Bay
2. Andrew Haydon Park
3. Britannia
4. Champlain Bridge-Remic Rapids
5. Ile Lemieux-Chaudiere Rapids
6. Vincent Massey Park
7. Central Experimental Farm
8. Bourget-Flooded agricultural fields, waterfowl staging area
9. Mer Bleue Bog
10. Rockcliffe Park
11. Lower Duck Island
12. Stony Swamp Conservation Area
13. Gatineau Park
14. Old Chelsea Ravine
15. Champlain Lookout-Eardley Escarpment

Sewage ponds provide excellent habitat for many birds. Here, dabbling ducks raise their young, swallows forage above the water for the multitudes of newly hatched insects, and shorebirds probe the mud for invertebrates. During migration, sewage ponds can attract hundreds of shorebirds and waterfowl.

The wet, boggy areas south of Ottawa are a haven for birds and other wildlife. Snipe are constantly displaying in spring, their spectacular aerial displays occurring high above the wetland. Bitterns lurk in the reeds and a blackbird aggressively defends its territory by displaying its broad, red shoulder patches.

One of the best places to birdwatch in Ottawa is at Britannia. Mud Lake, the adjacent woods, and the Ottawa River itself host ducks, herons, swallows and a variety of songbirds. If you can visit only one area, make it Britannia.

The marginal farmland and hobby farms around the Capital provide habitats for a variety of birds. The old fence lines, hedgerows, and overgrown fields are excellent areas to find kingbirds, House Wrens, Mourning Doves, Bobolinks and meadowlarks.

A typical Ottawa back yard. The shrubs and trees of different heights and densities duplicate the more natural conditions found in the wild. In this habitat, Northern Orioles will nest in the tall trees and Cedar Waxwings, American Robins, Blue Jays and Chipping Sparrows will be right at home.

BIRDS OF OTTAWA

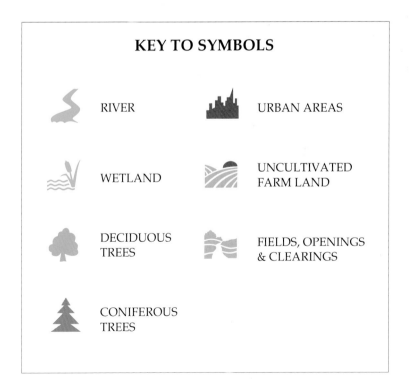

KEY TO SYMBOLS

RIVER

URBAN AREAS

WETLAND

UNCULTIVATED
FARM LAND

DECIDUOUS
TREES

FIELDS, OPENINGS
& CLEARINGS

CONIFEROUS
TREES

AMERICAN BITTERN

Botaurus lentiginosus
Butor d'Amérique
larger than crow-sized

THE AMERICAN BITTERN has a most unusual voice: a loud, guttural, three-syllable *pump-er-lunk* which can be heard from wetlands for a considerable distance. Its voice is often described as sounding like an old-fashioned water pump, a characteristic sound emanating from marshes in spring.

An expert at fishing, its overall brown colour pattern is excellent camouflage against the marsh vegetation, the bird seemingly frozen with bill outstretched, like an old stake sticking out from the mud.

When feeding, the bird stands motionless along the edge of a shallow pond, eyes concentrating on the water. Then, with amazing speed, the bill is thrust downward to seize the prey, be it a fish, crayfish, frog or snail.

The nest, built by the female, is a platform of dead marsh vegetation placed within the cattails. The four to six eggs are olive-brown to olive-buff and hatch after about 24 days of incubation. The young leave the nest when they are about 14 days old.

The cattail marshes at Ramsayville Marsh along Anderson Road or any area dominated by cattails, even those in roadside ditches, are excellent places to find this bird.

GREAT BLUE HERON

Ardea herodias
Grand Héron
larger than gull-sized

WE OFTEN INCORRECTLY CALL our largest heron a crane, but this inhabitant of shallow marshes and ponds around the city is not related to the crane family.

Great Blue Herons are most often sighted after the breeding season when the adults and immatures can be seen standing motionless waiting for a frog, fish or anything else that their spear-like bills can snare.

They nest near the tops of trees in colonies of varying sizes. The flattish nest is large, and built of sticks, and several nests may be located in one tree.

This bird must have secluded, undisturbed areas to nest, and wetland areas to feed from. Absence of either will cause the species to decline in number. As well, human intrusion into the breeding colonies can cause young herons to panic and jump from their nests, resulting in their deaths.

This bird can be found near ponds, streams, or along the quieter portions of the Ottawa River. The natural area around the Britannia filtration plant (Mud Lake) is a good spot for this species within the city.

CANADA GOOSE

Branta canadensis
Bernache du Canada
larger than gull-sized

THIS WELL KNOWN SYMBOL of wilderness and seasonal change is known to all of us. The magnificent Canada Goose is a familiar and thrilling sight — the sound of honking drifts down to the ground from their V-shaped formations to announce the arrival of spring or the onslaught of winter.

The family ties of Canada Geese are legendary. Believed to mate for life, an adult only seeks another mate upon the death of its partner. At the nest site, the gander is ever-vigilant, standing on guard to defend against all intrusions, including humans. Young geese migrate as a family group with their parents in the fall and return with them in the spring, leaving their parents only after they arrive at the nesting grounds. The young, now called yearlings, do not nest but gather in flocks with other yearlings. Canada Geese are one of the few bird species that stay in the family group after the nesting season.

Canada Geese migrate through the capital area in huge numbers. Vast flocks may be seen in the spring on the flooded cropland east of the city near Bourget. The river area in the west end of the city is a good place to look for them in autumn.

GREEN-WINGED TEAL

Anas crecca
Sarcelle à ailes vertes
smaller than crow-sized

OUR SMALLEST DUCK, the Green-winged Teal can be distinguished from all other ducks, except the Blue-winged Teal, by size alone. The male's handsome head markings and the lack of any blue in the forewing distinguish it from the Blue-winged. Unlike the Blue-winged, this species is rarely found in association with human habitation.

The Green-winged Teal breeds throughout Canada and it is one of the most widespread species in the country. It appears to have expanded its breeding range in Southern Ontario, taking advantage of the habitat created by sewage lagoons or other water impoundments.

The nest, a deep depression in a clump of grass or by a shrub, can be some distance from water. The ten to twelve white to pale olive-buff eggs are incubated by the female. When she leaves the nest, the nest and eggs are covered with down, making it difficult for predators to locate. The male, in the meantime, has abandoned the female and can be some kilometres away from the nest site to begin his molt.

Britannia, Shirleys Bay and other areas along the river are good places to view this species.

AMERICAN BLACK DUCK

Anas rubripes
Canard noir
gull-sized

BLACK DUCKS ARE FAIRLY COMMON throughout the year along the river. They are darker than the Mallard and lack the Mallard's white outer tail feathers and wing bars. In flight, the white underwings of the Black Duck provide a vivid contrast to its dark body. Mallards and Black Ducks freely hybridize and many of the birds will exhibit characteristics of both species.

The preferred nesting zone of the Black Duck is in the mixed-wood forest of the Canadian Shield where beaver ponds are a favourite habitat. Its nest is usually on the ground where the nine to ten eggs are incubated by the female. Blacks nest in a variety of habitats: nest sites can also be found in the tops of muskrat houses or tree cavities. In our region look for this bird along the river and in marshes. Some pass the winter here as well.

The diet of the Black ranges from aquatic vegetation, insects and their larvae, to small frogs and tadpoles. Being a dabbler, the bird feeds in shallow water where it reaches bottom by tipping up its tail and probing the mud with its bill.

MALLARD
Anas platyrhynchos
Canard colvert
gull-sized

THE MALLARD is the most common and best known duck in the Ottawa region. It is readily adaptable to urban areas from city parks to sewage lagoons, while in wilder places it frequents ponds, marshes, lakes and rivers. It can be quite tame in city areas but very wary in the wild.

The diet of the Mallard is varied. A dabbling duck, it up-ends while feeding, unlike diving ducks which, as their name implies, dive for their food. Mallards feed on aquatic vegetation, seeds, grain, insects and, in the city, on the handouts of people. A high protein diet, derived from invertebrates, is needed in early spring in order for the hens to be in good condition for egg laying.

Mallards nest on the ground. The nest, which contains up to fifteen dullish green eggs, is generally near water although it may be located some distance from it.

Young Mallard broods may appear as early as mid-May but should the first nesting attempt fail, a second effort is usually made. Broods can thus be readily observed until mid-summer. After breeding, the male Mallard abandons the female, leaving her to care for the young.

BLUE-WINGED TEAL

Anas discors
Sarcelle à ailes bleues
smaller than crow-sized

THIS SWIFT-FLYING SPECIES is highly migratory, wintering as far south as South America. Blue-wings are the first ducks to leave in the fall and, in the spring, are the last to return.

Blue-winged Teal are common spring and fall migrants in our region. During the breeding season, they are fairly common residents of the marshes and small ponds. Because of their late arrival from the wintering grounds, they are among the last dabbling ducks to nest but make up for this by nesting within a week of their arrival. Grassy areas are preferred for nesting and nests have been found as far as one mile away from water. Nine to twelve buff-white eggs are generally laid. Egg-laying can start when nest building has barely commenced. Ponds with adjacent grassy areas are favourite sites for this bird in rural areas.

This diminutive duck in its handsome breeding plumage gives a splash of colour in spring. The white facial crescent of the male contrasts with its steel-blue head and neck, a unique feature for identification. In flight a blue shoulder patch is visible on the wing, hence its common name.

Britannia, Ottawa Beach and Shirleys Bay are all excellent spots to see this species.

COMMON GOLDENEYE

Bucephala clangula
Garrot à oeil d'or
crow-sized

COMMON GOLDENEYE are characteristic ducks of the boreal forest in Ontario, where they nest in tree cavities. Their northern breeding range is only limited by the availability of trees large enough to have cavities of sufficient size to allow the duck to nest. The nest cavity can be as high as 20 metres from the ground. On average, ten pale bluish-green eggs are laid. When the young hatch, they remain in the cavity only a day or two, then they jump up from the nest to the edge of the cavity and flutter down uninjured to the mother below. She gathers her brood and leads them away.

Some people call these ducks "whistlers," a name derived from the whistling sound the birds make while in flight. This is not a vocalization but is caused by the air passing through the birds' wings.

Expert divers, goldeneyes can remain underwater for an average of thirty seconds at a time, and can reach a depth of about six metres in their search for food.

This species can easily be seen in the fast-flowing water areas of the Ottawa River from October to April. Viewpoints from the Champlain Bridge, Bate Island, Île Lemieux or Brébeûf Park are among the best within the Capital area.

COMMON MERGANSER
Mergus merganser
Grand Bec-scie
larger than crow-sized

THE COOL, SPARKLING WATERS of the lakes and rivers in the Canadian Shield are favoured by this species during the breeding season. Anyone who spends time in cottage country or regions like Algonquin Park will see this expert diving duck. The drake, with its blackish green head and black and whitish body, is vividly coloured and the hen, although drab in comparison, has a noticeable crest and a handsome tawny brown head.

The Common Merganser is a fish-eater, and its long serrated bill is an excellent aid in catching prey while swimming underwater.

Common Mergansers, which are the largest inland duck found in North America, usually nest in tree cavities but sometimes use ledges or nest on the ground under dense tangles of bushes. Like goldeneyes, young mergansers leave the tree cavity by fluttering to the ground. The young can dive soon after hatching. It is not uncommon for broods to mix into groups of twenty or more and be attended by several females.

This species is a regular wintering duck in our region, found in the open fast water areas of the Ottawa River.

Inset: female

30

RED-TAILED HAWK

Buteo jamaicensis
Buse à queue rousse
larger than crow-sized

THIS SPLENDID BIRD can often be seen soaring effortlessly, its reddish-brown tail highlighted against the sky. Around undeveloped fields, the Red-tailed Hawk can be seen perched on an exposed tree limb or fence post waiting for an unwary mouse or vole to give itself away and become the meal of the day. Although they prefer rodents, Red-tails will occasionally feed on pigeons in the city, as well as on injured or unsuspecting waterfowl.

The favoured habitat for Red-tails is open country mixed with woodlands: the woodlands are used for nesting; and the open country, for hunting. This patchwork pattern of landscape occurs frequently in many of the settled regions of Southern Ontario and thus the bird is common here and widely distributed.

A Red-tail usually builds its large, bulky stick-nest in the crotch of a deciduous tree, or occasionally in a white pine. Before the leaves are fully opened, the nest stands out from the tree tops. The two to four eggs are incubated mainly by the female, with the male making frequent visits to the nest to feed her. It is believed that the pair mates for life or until the death of one member of the pair.

AMERICAN KESTREL

Falco sparverius
Crécerelle d'Amérique
larger than robin-sized

THE AMERICAN KESTREL is the smallest and most common North American falcon, and it competes with the Red-tailed Hawk as the most common and widely distributed hawk in Ontario.

The female is larger than the male and has brown wings, whereas the male's wings are blue-gray. They prefer to nest in old woodpecker holes or hollows in trees but in the city they will use holes in walls or under roof gables, and will readily lay the four to six creamy brown splotched eggs in nest boxes. The male provides all the food for the female during the 30-day incubation period, and for the family for the 30-odd days before the young leave the nest.

We can often see this bird hovering over fields while hunting for mice, grasshoppers or crickets. Both along rural roads and in the city, Kestrels can be seen on telephone lines, fence posts and light standards.

In the city during winter, Kestrels prey mainly on small birds. The sudden explosion of House Sparrows away from your feeder may well be caused by a Kestrel looking for a meal.

PEREGRINE FALCON

Falco peregrinus
Faucon pèlerin
crow-sized

THIS STREAMLINED, POWERFUL BIRD is not one that you may think of as an urban bird. But thanks to the efforts of wildlife agencies and dedicated individuals working to save the species from extinction, re-introductions have been made in both Ottawa and Hull.

In its natural habitat, the Peregrine builds its nest on cliff faces, frequently in the vicinity of large bird colonies. That food supply is replaced in urban areas by an abundance of pigeons and House Sparrows which are no match for one of the fastest flying birds in the world.

A Peregrine will nest in a city, often on a ledge of a tall building. Here, its three to five eggs are laid, and incubated by both sexes for up to 35 days.

Virtually wiped out by DDT in eastern North America, the Peregrine is making a slow recovery in both cities and wild places of Canada and the United States. The continued use of DDT in Central America still poses a threat to its survival.

Peregrines were always rare and to see one engage in its spectacular aerial pursuits of prey will not be soon forgotten.

GRAY PARTRIDGE
Perdix perdix
Perdrix grise
larger than crow-sized

SOMETIMES CALLED A HUNGARIAN PARTRIDGE or a Hun, this bird is plump with short, rounded wings and a short tail. The bird presents an overall grey appearance underneath, with chestnut bars on its flanks and a flashy orange tail. The male possesses an obvious chestnut abdominal patch.

The nest is a hollow scrape in the ground located in some weedy corner of a farm field or similar sheltered area. Up to 20 eggs can be laid with the young hatching after about 23 to 25 days. Hungarian Partridge nests are hard to find as the female covers the nest when she leaves. Partridge nests can be inadvertently destroyed during haying operations as many nests are still being incubated during that time.

In the Capital region, Gray Partridges inhabit agricultural areas, open grasslands and weedy fields. They are permanent residents and can congregate in large flocks during the winter months. This species demonstrates a trend of peaking in numbers every few years. As a result, some years it is difficult to find Huns, and other years they are very common.

Some good areas for viewing are the cultivated fields and manure piles of the Experimental Farm and the areas south of the airport.

SORA

Porzana carolina
Râle de Caroline
robin-sized

THE FAR-CARRYING DESCENDING WHINNY of the Sora makes the bird's presence known in the marshes of our region. It often calls its own name.

Soras are the most widespread rail in Ontario, but availability of appropriate habitat is the key to the presence of this bird. Continued human disturbance and destruction of the wetlands could threaten the existence of the Sora.

The nest, often situated along the edge of a densely vegetated wetland, is a small loosely woven basket attached to standing stalks of marsh vegetation a few inches above the water, or constructed on the ground. Eight to thirteen buffy eggs, spotted with brown, are laid.

Rails are expert skulkers who move within the marsh vegetation with great dexterity. If disturbed, they frequently prefer to run within the vegetation rather than to fly.

A Sora can be best seen by sitting quietly near the edge of a marsh. The bird will appear along the muddy edge where it steps daintily along the mud. Its long toes allow it to walk nimbly across waterlily pads.

In summer, they eat many aquatic insects as well as small mollusks. Later in the summer, seeds are often eaten. Strong fliers, Soras have one of the longest migration routes of the rail family, wintering throughout the Caribbean area.

AMERICAN COOT

Fulica americana
Foulque d'Amérique
smaller than crow-sized

COOTS CAN BE NOISY BIRDS, their loud *coo-coo-coo-coo* echoing across the marshes day and night. Grunts, whistles, croaks, and babbling sounds accompanied by much splashing and splattering across the water give ample reason for the phrase, "crazy as a coot."

In our region, the birds seem to prefer large marshes with broad expanses of deeper open water, such as those found at Shirleys Bay. In early spring they are among the earliest water birds to return from their wintering grounds in the southern United States.

While feeding, coots can tip up like dabbling ducks in shallow waters yet they are expert divers which seek various aquatic plants or small fishes or tadpoles. Coots bob their heads while swimming, a habit that is a distinctive field mark.

The bird is semi-colonial in its nesting habits: a number of pairs are often located in the same vicinity. The nest is constructed by both sexes. Usually well concealed, it is built with the stems of marsh plants upon a platform of the same material, and it floats on the water, anchored to emergent plants.

The downy chicks are black with bristle-like orange to red down about the head, neck and shoulders. That colouration together with a bright red, black-tipped bill gives the young coots a clown-like, spectacular appearance.

KILLDEER
Charadrius vociferus
Pluvier kildir
robin-sized

OF ALL THE SHOREBIRDS found in Ontario, the Killdeer is the most familiar. It is found in virtually every open area including pastures, agricultural fields, stream banks and rooftops within the city itself. One can find the bird nesting on golf courses, airports, lawns, or on transportation and utility rights-of-way.

Like most shorebirds, Killdeer nest in a mere shallow depression in the ground, lined with a few pebbles and weeds. Usually, four light buff eggs blotched with black are laid.

Killdeers are famous for their elaborate distraction display. This crippled bird act is designed to lead intruders away from the nest or young. The bird moves away from the intruder dragging its tail or wing as if broken, sometimes tumbling to appear helpless. If you follow it, the act will continue, always just out of reach, until you are a considerable distance from the nest. The distraction display is most likely to occur just prior to the eggs hatching, or when the young have recently hatched.

Killdeer are one of the first species to return in spring: one can hear their raucous, persistent calls often when only patches of bare ground are visible.

SPOTTED SANDPIPER

Actitis macularia
Chevalier branlequeue
smaller than robin-sized

SPOTTED SANDPIPERS AND KILLDEERS probably share the title of the most widely distributed shorebirds in North America. Like other species which are widespread, Spotted Sandpipers are highly adaptable to a variety of habitats. You can find the bird along stream banks, edges of ponds and lake shorelines as well as in human-altered environments such as agricultural fields and sewage lagoons.

When in breeding plumage, the adults have black dots on their white undersides which contrast with their greyish-brown backs. In autumn, the spots are absent.

This common sandpiper appears like a nervous bird with its constant teetering. It bobs its tail almost continuously as it searches for insects along the shore. In flight, the wings are held very stiffly and the wing beats are shallow, giving the appearance of a jerky, nervous flight.

The well hidden nest is a depression in the ground. The male provides most of the incubation and care for the young. Hatching occurs after 20 to 22 days and in late nests, the female may assist in the incubation of the four buffy, spotted brown eggs. As soon as the young hatch, they can run over the ground, bobbing and teetering in a manner similar to their parents.

Look for this sandpiper wherever shorelines exist.

SEMIPALMATED SANDPIPER

Calidris pusilla
Bécasseau semipalmé
larger than sparrow-sized

THESE COMMON SANDPIPERS do not nest within our region but they can be found in large numbers during migration in spring and fall. They are the most abundant sandpiper during this period and possibly the most abundant of all shorebirds within their range. They gather in compact flocks, their bodies almost touching, as they probe the mud for worms or aquatic insects. The name "semipalmated" describes the webbing between the front toes of these birds.

This bird is one of the more difficult species of sandpiper to identify. It is similar to several other small shorebird species that are collectively known as "peeps." It is sparrow-sized with black legs and a short bill. The female is slightly larger than the male. Experience and comparison with other similar species are the only ways of distinguishing it.

Visit muddy shorelines and marvel at the large flocks whirling through the air, twisting and turning simultaneously in tight formations: never a bird hesitates in determining the direction of the flight. On the ground when resting, they huddle together, each bird's bill tucked into its wing, the bird often standing on one leg.

Sewage ponds, and muddy shorelines of the river are good places to see this species.

COMMON SNIPE

Gallinago gallinago
Bécassine des marais
larger than robin-sized

THE COMMON SNIPE is a large, brown striped shorebird with a spectacularly long bill, used for probing in the mud for a variety of small animals. It is probably best known for its spring courtship flights above the breeding grounds. These flights, which begin in April, are incredible displays: the bird will dive from a height at which it seems a mere speck in the sky, making a winnowing sound by extending its tail feathers so they vibrate as the air rushes through them.

The bird prefers wet, boggy areas that provide both soft mud for feeding and cover for nesting. The nest is a scrape on a piece of dry ground where four variably-coloured eggs are laid. If you happen upon a Snipe's nest, it is important not to disturb it. Snipes are particularly sensitive to human contact, and often abandon their nests even after only a slight disturbance.

Watch and listen for this bird in the spring evening sky. They also like elevated perches and you may see them on roadside fenceposts which they frequently use for that purpose. Mer Bleue, the Moodie Drive area, and Shirley's Bay are three areas where the bird can often be seen.

RING-BILLED GULL

Larus delawarensis
Goéland à bec cerclé
larger than crow-sized

OVER THE PAST SEVERAL YEARS, Ring-billed Gulls have undergone a population explosion. New colonies have become established in urban and industrial areas to such an extent that they are viewed by many as a pest species. Ring-billed Gulls are opportunistic; that is, they take advantage of the many human-created food sources and are adaptable to a variety of habitats. They nest on breakwaters, slag heaps and industrial areas. In the Capital region, huge nesting colonies can be seen on the islands in the Chaudière Rapids and from Ile Lemieux.

The nest of a Ring-billed Gull is built on the ground where two to three buffy eggs with various brown spots and blotches are laid. The young learn to swim at an early age, so they can take to the water to escape intruders.

The large and rapid population increase has created many problems, from damaged crops to spoiled recreation areas. Control programs have been instituted at some nesting sites in an attempt to reduce the problem. However, gulls can also be beneficial: they eat large numbers of grasshoppers and are useful scavengers.

HERRING GULL

Larus argentatus
Goéland argenté
gull-sized

THIS IS THE COMMON large "sea gull" of our region, its name alluding to the fish which forms part of its varied diet. The Great Lakes provide a bounteous food resource in the form of alewives, a species of fish that flourishes in our polluted environment. Herring Gulls have also adapted to human garbage as a source of food.

The adult Herring Gull has a blue-grey mantle with black wing-tips. Its legs are flesh-coloured and at close range, you can see a red dot near the tip of its yellow bill. The Ring-billed Gull is similar but smaller, with yellowish legs and a black ring near the tip of the bill. These two gulls are common in our area and can often be seen at very close range in park or waterfront areas.

Herring Gulls utilize a variety of nest sites from undisturbed islands in the Great Lakes, recreational lakes and rivers, to various types of shorelines. Generally, they nest in the same colonies year after year, although they occasionally nest in single pairs. The nest, on the ground, is lined with grass or other vegetation, and two to three eggs of variable colour are laid. Immature Herring Gulls obtain full adult plumage after three years of moults.

COMMON TERN
Sterna hirundo
Sterne pierregarin
smaller than crow-sized

COMMON TERNS nest throughout Ontario, usually in colonies, both in wild areas and human environments. Natural nesting sites can be small sparsely vegetated islands or gravel beaches. Terns will also nest on slag heaps, dredge spoil sites and even structures like piers or breakwaters.

The nest is a shallow depression in the sand and gravel where usually two to three eggs are laid. Although the bird tolerates some vegetation, when the plants spread and grow too much the nest site is abandoned.

While foraging for food a tern can hover above the water with rapid wingbeats. When it spots a school of small fish, it swiftly dives and snatches its prey from the water.

Common Terns can easily be confused with another tern species, the Arctic Tern, which occurs in Ontario in small numbers. Arctic Terns can sometimes be seen migrating up the Ottawa River en route to their Arctic breeding grounds. They can appear much whiter in the wing, and fly in a straight unwavering line. Common Terns have darker wing tips and more orange colour in their bills, and appear in loose, more casual flocks over the river.

BLACK TERN

Chlidonias niger
Guifette noire
robin-sized

THIS GRACEFUL BIRD is one of the most handsome birds in the tern family. Breeding season adults have dark black heads and necks with slate-grey backs, wings and tails.

Black Terns spend much time in the air, hovering buoyantly above the marsh where, swallow-like, they snatch insects from the air. On shallow dives into the water, they pluck small fishes from beneath the surface.

This species has very specific habitat requirements. Nests are constructed in cattail marshes or shallow, weedy areas of inland lakes and rivers. The birds nest in loose colonies in semi-open areas where the emergent vegetation is neither too dense or too thin, and where water depth is just right.

The nest is built of dead vegetation on floating mats of vegetation; sometimes a muskrat house may be used. Two to three eggs, olive or buff with heavy brown markings, are laid, and incubation is 21 to 22 days. The young are able to leave the nest a few days after hatching but they are vigorously defended by the parents. Intruders into a nesting site will be greeted with shrill cries and repeated dive-bombing attacks from the adults, a behaviour common to all of the tern family.

ROCK DOVE

Columba livia
Pigeon biset
smaller than crow-sized

THE ROCK DOVE, or domestic pigeon, needs no introduction. This ubiquitous bird is found in every city, town and farm. A Eurasian species, it was domesticated and first introduced into North America by the French at Port Royal, Nova Scotia in 1606.

In the Old World, when in the natural environment, Rock Doves used caves and cliffs for their nest sites. In cities, they use the ledges of older houses and modern commercial structures. The ability to readily adapt to the human environment has allowed the species to become firmly established throughout many parts of the world. That ability, plus the fact that Rock Doves will have two or three families a year and can nest in any month, helps to explain the success of this species.

The nests are flimsily constructed of sticks or twigs, and contain two white eggs. When the young hatch, they are fed "pigeon milk," a substance produced in the crop of the parents. When older, pigeons eat seeds, garbage, crusts and some berries.

Rock Doves exhibit a great deal of variation in their colour pattern; some indeed can be quite handsome. They are also one of the swiftest birds in flight.

MOURNING DOVE

Zenaida macroura
Tourterelle triste
smaller than crow-sized

THE PERCEIVED SADNESS of the bird's call has given the Mourning Dove its name. Its distinctive mellow cooing can be heard from some distance.

Mourning Doves are common in the woodlots and fields of our rural areas. However, any city neighbourhood with adequate cover may house a pair: they will often nest in a tree in a yard.

The nest is flimsy, made of small twigs in the form of a loose platform. The two pure white eggs are incubated for fifteen days, then the young hatch and are at first fed "pigeon milk." Later, the parents regurgitate seeds to feed the young.

This bird can easily be found, as it has a habit of perching in the open on wires, TV antennas, poles or on the ground along roadsides, where it seeks gravel to aid in its digestion. One can distinguish it from a Rock Dove by its sleeker appearance and long, pointed tail.

Given adequate food and shelter, Mourning Doves can remain in the region throughout the winter months. Keep your bird feeder full, for the doves can brighten up a dreary winter day.

GREAT HORNED OWL

Bubo virginianus
Grand-duc d'Amérique
larger than gull-sized

THIS LARGE OWL is the most familiar of the owls in Ontario. It can be found within the wooded areas of the Capital where its soft hooting can be heard as early as January.

Great Horned Owls nest in February or early March. Old hawk or crow nests are often chosen but the same nest is not always used each year. Once the young have hatched, parental care continues for some months. Young birds remain in the nest for about 50 days, and then, still being nearly flightless, they spend a few weeks on the ground or low branches in the nesting territory, being tended by the parents.

Savage and powerful, the Great Horned Owl has no natural predators to fear; humans are its only formidable foe. The owl is an opportunistic feeder, attempting to catch any animal or bird that presents itself. Rabbits, mice, squirrels, skunks, grouse and ducks are among its varied menu. It will even tackle a porcupine.

The undigestible portion of food eaten by an owl is regurgitated in the form of pellets. The fur, feathers and bones contained in the pellet can be identified giving us data on the bird's diet.

47

SNOWY OWL

Nyctea scandiaca
Harfang des neiges
larger than gull-sized

THIS SPECIES IS ONE of the most distinctive owls. A resident of the Arctic tundra of both North America and Old World regions, it may be found in our area only during the winter months.

When wintering here, it frequents locales that are outwardly similar to the barren, open country of the tundra. Snowy Owls can be found in the open agricultural land surrounding the city, especially in fields where rodents abound. They often perch on fence posts, hay bales, lone trees, or other elevated areas while watching for mice and other mammals during daylight hours.

Snowy Owls possess a luxurious feather coat which protects them from the extreme cold. Feathers also cover their feet to the tips of the toes. These owls are so well feathered that only their yellow eyes are fully exposed.

This powerful bird is one of the largest and heaviest of our owls. The adult male can be almost pure white but the female is more darkly barred. Immature birds are darker yet. Females are larger than the males.

NORTHERN SAW-WHET OWL

Aegolius acadicus
Petite Nyctale
larger than sparrow-sized

THE SAW-WHET OWL is the smallest owl found in eastern Canada. Active from dusk through the night hours, Saw-whets are motionless and appear tame during the day. Finding one, however, is difficult as they roost in dense tangles of cover like alders and cedars, or in tree cavities.

Breeding distribution for the species is the most dense in southern Ontario ,where it is found in the mixed coniferous and deciduous woodlands of the Canadian Shield. The bird nests in old woodpecker holes or natural tree cavities, with egg laying commencing in early April. Five or six white eggs are laid and are incubated primarily by the female.

Early in the breeding season, Saw-whets call frequently. They possess a variety of calls, one of which resembles the filing noise of a saw, hence the name. Its most common call is a monotonous series of clear, metallic-like notes, repeated incessantly. After nesting has begun, the birds become quiet.

The diet of the Northern Saw-whet Owl consists of mice and smaller mammals like chipmunks or red squirrels. Insects are eaten, too, and an occasional small bird.

Saw-whet Owls closely resemble the Boreal Owl in appearance. Look for the black bill and streaked forehead of the Saw-whet, should you have the good luck to see one at close range.

COMMON NIGHTHAWK

Chordeiles minor
Engoulevent d'Amérique
larger than robin-sized

MOST OFTEN HEARD OR SEEN on warm, summer evenings over the cities and towns of southern Ontario, the Common Nighthawk is one of our more familiar summer birds. Even downtown, the birds frequent the night sky just above streetlamp level, oblivious to the noise and confusion below as they feed on the hordes of insects attracted by the lights.

As it sweeps the insects out of the air, the nighthawk flies in a graceful but highly erratic manner. Often the bird utters a distinctive nasal *peent* call as it flies. During courtship, it engages in spectacular aerial displays, making steep nose-dives that sometimes end in a muffled boom sound created by the air rushing through its wings.

In a more natural environment, nighthawks can nest on the ground in the open, gravelly soil of pastures and other clearings. In cities and towns, flat gravelled roofs provide ideal nesting areas. The multitude of insects attracted by the city lights provide ample food, as well, so nighthawks have been able to adapt easily to the urban environment.

CHIMNEY SWIFT

Chaetura pelagica
Martinet ramoneur
smaller than sparrow-sized

THE CHIMNEY SWIFT is a sooty grey-coloured bird with long, narrow wings. It can often be seen above our city skyline: its silhouette resembles a "flying cigar" with wings engaged in a constant jerky motion.

Swifts are well named, for their flight is indeed rapid: they zig-zag across the sky at heights that range from just above our homes, to levels that make them appear to be mere specks. While in flight, they constantly utter a "skittering" call which can be readily heard on the ground. All food is caught on the wing, and the swift gets water by touching the water surface lightly with its bill. Even nesting material is snapped off as the bird hovers close to a twig.

The birds do utilize chimneys for nesting and as places to roost. The chimneys of large homes in our older residential neighbourhoods are ideal for this purpose. While roosting, swifts cling with their sharp nails to the chimney walls. In large groups their bodies may overlap each other like rows of shingles. When nesting, usually one pair will use a smaller house chimney. The nest is cemented together and attached to the wall by the glutenous saliva of the birds. The young first fly thirty days after hatching and return to the nest after the first flight.

51

RUBY-THROATED HUMMINGBIRD

Archilochus colubris
Colibri à gorge rubis
smaller than sparrow-sized

THE RUBY-THROATED HUMMINGBIRD is the smallest bird found in Ontario, its body probably no longer than the end joint of your thumb. Because of its small size, the Ruby-throat has the highest metabolism of any warm-blooded vertebrate animal in the world; therefore it must feed continuously in the daytime to stay alive.

Hummingbirds feed on minute insects and nectar obtained from brightly coloured flowers, which they reach into with their long tongues. In addition, hummingbirds are attracted to the sap oozing from drill holes of the Yellow-bellied Sapsucker. This bird can be found in any garden, woodland clearing or forest edge, feeding on a variety of flower species including wild plants like fireweed and jewelweed, and many common garden plants, such as columbine, honeysuckle and salvia. You can easily develop a backyard garden of colourful flowers with various blooming periods that will attract the bird. As well, they feed readily at hummingbird feeders, usually red-coloured vials filled with a solution of one part sugar to four parts of water.

BELTED KINGFISHER

Ceryle alcyon
Martin-pêcheur d'Amérique
larger than robin-sized

THE BELTED KINGFISHER is the only species of Kingfisher found in Canada. A conspicuous bird, we often hear its harsh rattling call before we see it. It cries out as it swiftly flies below the treetops, following the course of a stream. Sometimes the bird hovers above the water, watching for prey.

Commonly seen near water, a kingfisher can perch motionless on a dead limb above the water for long periods. When a small fish is sighted, the bird dives directly into the water, seizing the fish below the surface in its strong bill. It will later disgorge pellets of undigestible food items like fish bones and scales.

Kingfishers excavate long horizontal burrows into eroded river or lake banks for nesting. Sometimes the bird will select an artificial site such as a gravel pit or a road or railway cutback, as long as the location is close to water. The bird digs the hole with its bill then pushes the soil out with its feet: it may take the bird up to three weeks to dig the burrow, depending on the type of soil in the bank. Usually six or seven eggs are laid, which are then incubated primarily by the female.

YELLOW-BELLIED SAPSUCKER

Sphyrapicus varius
Pic maculé
smaller than robin-sized

SAP IS AN IMPORTANT FOOD SOURCE for the Yellow-bellied Sapsucker, but a variety of insects are also eaten, including forest tent caterpillars. This bird drills rows of small holes about 0.5 cm in diameter. When the sap begins to flow and fills the shallow holes, the sapsucker uses its long, brush-tipped tongue to lick up the sap, and the insects on it. The holes also attract hummingbirds and warblers.

Sapsuckers are found in second growth forest where there is a preponderance of white birch and poplar. Birch is favoured for its sweet sap, and poplar for its soft inner core which is ideal for nest excavation. Usually the tree chosen for nesting is still alive, and its sapwood is still sound but the heartwood has begun to decay. The male does most of the nest excavation, and then about five or six white eggs are laid. Incubation is done by both species, with the male usually on the nest at night.

The bird is common in wooded areas of our region; however, it breeds most often around country estate lots or in the Gatineau Hills.

DOWNY WOODPECKER
Picoides pubescens
Pic mineur
sparrow-sized

DOWNY WOODPECKERS may be commonly found throughout the wooded areas of the city and are a welcome, frequent visitor to our backyard feeders in winter. Watch for them in ravines, woodlots and in older neighbourhoods where deciduous trees are established. Sometimes you can also find them in open fields searching on mullein stalks or drilling on goldenrod galls for insect larvae.

Although the Downy Woodpecker is seen often in winter, it goes into seclusion during the breeding season. Both sexes work to dig out a gourd-shaped nesting cavity, which may be as deep as twenty to thirty centimetres, in a dead tree or snag. Four to five white eggs are laid and after twelve days of incubation, the young hatch, and the feeding begins. The young have voracious appetites requiring the adults to feed them every two or three minutes.

This species is our smallest woodpecker and it is almost identical in plumage to the larger Hairy Woodpecker, which has a longer, heavier bill. The males of both species have a small red patch on the back of the head that is lacking on the females.

The long drumming of male woodpeckers, so often heard in spring, is a territorial pronouncement and also serves to attract males and females together in courtship.

NORTHERN FLICKER

Colaptes auratus
Pic flamboyant
larger than robin-sized

ONE OF OUR BEST KNOWN WOODPECKERS, the Northern Flicker is conspicuous because of its large white rump patch and yellow underwing linings. Its audible call, undulating flight and its habit of feeding on the ground are factors adding to its familiarity. Sexes look similar, but the adult female lacks the black moustache patch.

An adaptable species, flickers inhabit a variety of habitats but prefer the open, wooded areas of our parks or older residential neighbourhoods containing larger trees. They spend a lot of time on lawns, probing the ground for ants.

Northern Flickers nest in tree cavities and either excavate a new hole each year or use one from a previous year. Flickers will also use cavities in fence posts or telephone poles. The birds sometimes nest in boxes put up for them in backyards; however, competition by starlings for a box may be a problem. Most flicker nest sites can be viewed from a distance, making this species easy to observe during nesting.

Six to eight glossy white eggs are laid atop fresh woodchips in the cavity. After incubation by both sexes for about eleven or twelve days, the young hatch. The parents feed them by placing their bills into the yawning gapes of the young birds and regurgitating food.

PILEATED WOODPECKER

Dryocopus pileatus
Grand Pic
larger than crow-sized

A LOUD, POWERFUL CALL announces the presence of this bird. Its echoing drumming on a dead tree or stub advertises its territory but for such a large, noisy bird, it can be elusive.

The species prefers more extensive tracts of forests, but readily adapts to areas containing mature trees if unmolested. When established in a territory, the bird defends it against other Pileated Woodpeckers throughout the year. During the winter months, it may also visit the suet at your bird feeder.

The nest site is usually between 4.5 and 21 metres up from the ground and can sometimes be discovered by the pile of woodchips at the base of the tree. As with other species of woodpecker, the young are highly vocal and give the nest site away.

Pileated Woodpeckers chisel large vertical cavities in tree trunks in pursuit of food. They are sometimes accused of causing severe damage to trees or utility poles, but in fact they only "damage" wood already infested with carpenter ants.

Formerly much decreased in numbers, the species has made a comeback as second growth forests have matured. Watch for it, or its obvious signs, around the mature wooded areas of your neighbourhood, in cottage country in the Gatineau, or in the forests along Moodie Drive.

EASTERN WOOD PEWEE

Contopus virens
Pioui de l'Est
larger than sparrow-sized

THE EASTERN WOOD PEWEE is a common flycatcher of our open woodlands in urban parks and older neighbourhoods. It can be distinguished from other dull-coloured flycatchers by its larger size, and darker colouration. It lacks the obvious eye-ring of other flycatchers, but it has distinct wing bars.

An inhabitant of treetops, this bird is more often heard than seen. It has a distinctive song: a plaintive call of *pee-wee*, which drops in pitch, announces its presence. Even on the hottest, most humid days, pewees continue to call, long past the period when most birds have stopped singing for the day.

Pewees prefer the tall shady trees that are so common in our region. Open forest created by estate development in wooded areas, or in cottage country, has provided a habitat suitable for the bird.

It forages like other flycatchers, eating a wide variety of insect life. Some berries are also eaten in late summer.

This species seems to be ubiquitous. From the Experimental Farm to the summer cottage, the Eastern Wood Pewee is a part of the hot, summer Ontario scene.

LEAST FLYCATCHER

Empidonax minimus
Moucherolle tchébec
sparrow-sized

A DULL-COLOURED flycatcher, the Least is olive-grey above and white underneath. Although it is our smallest flycatcher, it is quite similar to several other species, even to the experienced eye. In the field it is best identified by its frequent *che-bec* call which is often repeated. Other flycatchers have their own distinctive calls.

Least Flycatchers are fairly common summer residents in second growth woodlands throughout the city and surrounding countryside. They like the woodland edge or forest openings, and can be seen in woodlots, city parks, or in mature, treed neighbourhoods.

The nest is usually built in the crotch of a branch in a small hardwood tree. Tall shrubs like alder, red osier dogwood and willow are also used. Four creamy white eggs are usually laid in a thin-walled cup nest. The female incubates the eggs for about 14 days, during which time she is sometimes fed by the male.

Like other flycatchers, the Least will perch on an exposed twig or post and dart out to catch passing insects. It also catches insects by scrambling about the bark and leaves of trees.

EASTERN PHOEBE

Sayornis phoebe
Moucherolle phébi
sparrow-sized

THIS BIRD IS BEST IDENTIFIED by its behaviour. When "singing" it calls its name quite distinctly, with the accent on the first syllable: *fee-be*, repeated over and over. This bird's most noticeable habit is that of "wagging" its tail, or sweeping it up and down repeatedly, when the bird alights on a perch.

Eastern Phoebes are one of the earliest birds to return in spring. They can appear as early as late March or early April.

The Phoebe is one of our hardiest flycatchers. While it passes through the city on migration, it is more common as a breeder in the greenbelt near water and, of course, throughout cottage country and the Gatineau Hills. The species nests largely on human structures such as old farmhouses, or on the beams of country road bridges or footbridges crossing small streams.

The five white eggs of this bird are laid in a bulky nest constructed of mud, leaves, grasses and other material. Sometimes the bird will construct a second nest on top of the old one or it may repair and re-use the former nest.

GREAT CRESTED FLYCATCHER

Myiarchus crinitus
Tyran huppé
smaller than robin-sized

AN INHABITANT OF WOODLAND EDGES and forest openings, the Great Crested Flycatcher is common throughout Southern Ontario from May to September. Look for this bird in woodlots both in and outside of the city. Neighbourhoods and parks with mature trees are also good locations.

The Great Crested frequents the upper branches of mature trees and spends much time foraging for insects in the tree canopy. Its loud *wheep* call is often heard but the bird can be hard to spot, obscured by the leaves of the tall trees. Like other flycatchers, it darts swiftly out from its perch to snatch dragonflies, moths, and other flying insects.

The species is a cavity nester in deciduous trees. It prefers natural cavities but also uses abandoned woodpecker holes. As well, Great Crested Flycatchers will nest in bird boxes provided for it. Within the cavity or birdbox, a cup-like nest is built of leaves, moss, grass, pine needles and other miscellaneous litter. Curiously, cast-off snake skins are often used.

Four to six creamy eggs with various handsome brownish patterns are incubated by the female, with the young hatching after thirteen to fifteen days.

EASTERN KINGBIRD
Tyrannus tyrannus
Tyran tritri
smaller than robin-sized

THE EASTERN KINGBIRD IS A PUGNACIOUS BIRD which fearlessly attacks crows, hawks, and other large birds that may pass through its territory. The intruders are often vigorously pursued for some distance until the Kingbird is satisfied that there is no threat to its territory.

A large flycatcher, it is conspicuous as it perches in open places on fences, posts, or exposed tree limbs. From there, it darts out to pick off its flying insect prey, often with an audible snap of its bill. Then the bird casually returns to its perch and sits alert, waiting for its next morsel.

Its short quick wingbeats appear to give the Kingbird a quivering appearance when in flight. It also is quite vocal, uttering many high-pitched notes.

In our region, Kingbirds are easily seen around farms, roadsides, old pasture fields or other open areas with scattered trees.

The nest of an Eastern Kingbird is built well out on a horizontal tree limb or sometimes in a shrub, dead snag, or stump. It commonly nests in flooded areas where dead snags abound. Often the nest is poorly concealed, as the bird probably relies on its aggressiveness to ward off intruders.

HORNED LARK

Eremophila alpestris
Alouette cornue
larger than sparrow-sized

THIS IS THE ONLY MEMBER of the lark family that is native to North America. In our region, the Horned Lark can be seen in areas of fallow land surrounding the city, pastures, and in open areas such as airfields. It has a high tinkling song, a welcome sound when you think that spring will never arrive. The bird sings from any slight elevation on the ground, or while in flight.

The majority of this bird's food consists of weed seeds, a food item prevalent in fallow fields and roadsides. Gathering in large groups, Horned Larks can be very conspicuous in winter as they descend upon one weed patch then flock to another.

The bird nests in dry, open spaces, in a depression on the ground. The nest is built of grasses and similar vegetation where three to five greyish eggs with large brown spots are laid. The eggs hatch after about eleven days of incubation. The young leave the nest before they are able to fly, but they are cared for by the parents for several more days.

The "horns" of the Horned Lark are small black feathers on the head, which are difficult to see.

PURPLE MARTIN

Progne subis
Hirondelle noire
larger than sparrow-sized

THE PURPLE MARTIN, our largest swallow, is a noisy, colonial nesting bird, which readily nests in apartment-style bird boxes provided for it. The provision of nestboxes has enabled the Purple Martin to be more widely distributed: in fact, records of the species nesting in natural conditions are almost unknown in Ontario.

The martin returns to the same nest box each year. Both sexes construct a nest of grasses, bark, leaves and other material in the compartment. Four to five dull white eggs are laid, with incubation being done by the female. After the young can fly, the martins abandon the nest and range more widely.

The Purple Martin feeds over water, marshes and open spaces catching a wide variety of flying insects; however, its legendary power at controlling mosquitoes is overrated.

We can help this bird by erecting martin houses in suitable open areas on top of poles five to six metres high. As House Sparrows and Starlings compete with Purple Martins for the nest box, the martin house should be taken down in fall and re-erected in late April when they return from the south.

Occasionally, cold, wet springs may decimate a Purple Martin colony. A prolonged period of poor weather can create a lack of flying insects, with starvation resulting.

TREE SWALLOW
Tachycineta bicolor
Hirondelle bicolore
sparrow-sized

THIS SPECIES IS the earliest swallow to return in spring. Often, a few birds are back by late March with the majority of the species arriving in early April, depending on the spring weather.

Tree Swallows nest in tree cavities, old woodpecker holes and bird boxes erected in suitable open habitat. Flooded wooded areas like those around beaver ponds, with abundant standing dead timber, are choice nesting sites. The bird will also tolerate close neighbours and it is not unusual for boxes to be occupied even when they are placed in relatively close proximity to each other.

A nest is constructed of grass and similar matter. Four to six white eggs are laid, with incubation being undertaken by both sexes for thirteen to sixteen days.

You can often see the Tree Swallow perching for long periods on the fence wire near the nest box. The bird flies into the box when intruders are nearby and at times, the intruders are greeted with vigorous chattering and aggressive diving as the swallow defends its nest. The Tree Swallow can also be seen flying gracefully over ponds, marshes and fields as it forages for insects.

BARN SWALLOW

Hirundo rustica
Hirondelle des granges
sparrow-sized

ONE OF THE MOST widely distributed bird species, the Barn Swallow nests not only throughout most of North America, but also in Europe and Asia, where the species is known simply as the Swallow.

The Barn Swallow gets its name from its nesting preference for barns, old houses, outbuildings or other structures. The birds may nest as single pairs or in loose colonies. There is a large colony of Barn and Cliff Swallows at the filtration plant buildings at Britannia.

Barn Swallows may take one to two weeks to construct their cup-shaped mud nest. The birds gather mud in their bills and plaster it upon a beam or wall, mixing some vegetation in with the mud. Four to six white eggs, spotted with reddish brown, are laid. The female does most of the incubation.

In August, swallows begin to gather in large numbers, on telephone wires and fence lines, but by September most have departed for their wintering grounds in South America.

BLUE JAY
Cyanocitta cristata
Geai bleu
robin-sized

THIS BOLD, RAUCOUS and strikingly handsome bird requires little description. The sentinel of the woods or of the neighbourhood, it announces its presence with its screaming call. Its voice is extremely varied, from its familiar *jay* call to soft, barely audible notes.

Although noisy for most of the year, it becomes quite silent during the nesting season; the opposite of most songbirds. The bulky nest, usually built in an evergreen, is constructed of sticks, moss and a variety of other items. Four to six greenish or bluish eggs dotted with spots of brown are laid. The female incubates the eggs for seventeen or eighteen days.

An inhabitant of mixed or deciduous woods, jays can be found practically everywhere. They have adapted well to the urban environment: our gardens with their ornamental shrubs and trees are much to their liking. In older neighbourhoods, Blue Jays especially like oaks and beech trees, as the fruits of these trees are a favourite food.

Blue Jays are omnivorous — they will eat almost anything. Nuts, berries, insects and birds' eggs are included in its diet. At feeders they especially love peanuts and sunflower seeds.

AMERICAN CROW

Corvus brachyrhynchos
Corneille d'Amérique
crow-sized

CROWS ARE WELL ADAPTED TO CITY LIFE and can often be found taking advantage of human rubbish, whether foraging through garbage cans in the local park or at landfill sites, or scouring whatever can be found in the lanes or streets. They also eat large numbers of insects and are a major predator of birds' eggs.

These birds prefer open areas for foraging, and wooded areas for roosting and nesting. The largest populations of crows can be found in the agricultural areas that surround the city, and in areas such as Gatineau Park, where the mix of woodlot and open space is ideally suited to their needs. Crows have benefitted immensely from human land use practices.

The American Crow is not protected by law and consequently the bird has been persecuted throughout the country. Despite this, it has maintained or increased its numbers, proof of the bird's resourcefulness.

The nest of this bird is a bulky assemblage of sticks lined with soft grass. Old nests are often refurbished and if used for a few years, they can become quite large. Four to six greenish-blue, brown-splotched eggs are laid, and incubated by both sexes.

COMMON RAVEN

Corvus corax
Grand Corbeau
gull-sized

THIS BIRD IS SIMILAR IN APPEARANCE to the American Crow but it is a much larger bird, with a big heavy bill. In flight, its round or wedge-shaped tail is a good field mark, as is the bird's tendency to soar like a hawk.

It is unlikely that you will see ravens within the city core but you can't miss them in Gatineau Park. A drive up the Parkway to the Champlain Lookout will normally provide a chance to see a raven or two as they soar on the updrafts created by the Eardley Escarpment.

Ravens use the cliff faces of this escarpment as nesting sites, and conifers are also sometimes selected. They are early nesters and aerial courtship displays start in February. The nests are large arrays of sticks lined with finer material in which three to five eggs are laid, beginning as early as April. A large pile of sticks and the tell-tale whitewash on the cliff face give the nest site away.

A variety of food is eaten by these birds including small mammals, birds and their eggs, but Ravens are largely scavengers.

69

BLACK-CAPPED CHICKADEE

Parus atricapillus
Mésange a tête noire
smaller than sparrow-sized

THE CHICKADEE is most obvious in winter, and is easily attracted to the bird feeder. Some individuals act tame and will flutter to your hand for a nut or sunflower seed.

Even on the coldest days, a seemingly deserted ravine or wooded area can be filled with the good-natured *chicka-dee-dee-dee* calls of a winter flock. Chickadees are constantly on the move as they search branches and bark for insect eggs; however, they do maintain specific winter territories. The flocks disband in early spring with one or two dominant males setting up breeding territories in the former winter flock area.

Chickadees nest in a tree cavity usually not far from the ground. They can select old woodpecker holes or natural cavities but generally the cavities are excavated by the chickadees themselves in rotten stumps or tree trunks. Soft materials line the cavity to form the nest, in which six to eight dull white and spotted eggs are laid. Chickadees tend to be secretive around the nest site: from egg laying until the young leave the nest, the birds are quiet.

In the winter, a great place to see chickadees is along Moodie Drive, where various bird feeders have been set up by the Ottawa Field Naturalists Club.

70

RED-BREASTED NUTHATCH

Sitta canadensis
Sittelle à poitrine rousse
smaller than sparrow-sized

WHITE-BREASTED NUTHATCH

Sitta carolinensis
Sittelle à poitrine blanche
sparrow-sized

NUTHATCHES HAVE A VERY DISTINCTIVE SHAPE and a habit of feeding head down as they move from the top of a tree trunk to the bottom, making them easy to identify. This odd feeding angle may have evolved to allow them to exploit the bark of trees for insect larvae that other birds may have missed. Their *anke-anke* call is also a good give-away to their presence.

Both species can be found in the city, but the White-breasted is more common. Large numbers of Red-breasted Nuthatches can be seen, however, in migration. The latter species is found in association with coniferous trees while the larger White-breasted Nuthatch is more common on deciduous trees. Both species will readily visit feeding stations.

Nuthatches nest in tree holes which they sometimes excavate themselves. The Red-breasted Nuthatch has the unusual habit of smearing pitch from coniferous trees around the nest hole entrance with its bill.

Red-breasted Nuthatch populations have increased in recent times, likely due to the proliferation of conifer plantations.

Top: Red-breasted Nuthatch
Bottom: White-breasted Nuthatch

BROWN CREEPER

Certhia americana
Grimpereau brun
smaller than sparrow-sized

THIS BROWN AND WHITE streaked bird creeps up the tree trunk searching bark crevices for insects with its long curved bill, while bracing itself with its tail propped against the trunk. When it reaches the top of a tree, it flies down to the bottom of the next one where it repeats the feeding process. This behaviour, together with a very high-pitched call, are often the only clues to the presence of a creeper, for its colouration is excellent camouflage against the bark.

Brown Creepers prefer mature woodlands of both hardwood and conifer. Flooded areas are especially favoured for the hanging bark of dead trees offers ideal sites for its crescent-shaped nest. On rare occasions the nest may be constructed in a tree cavity.

Uncommon in summer, the bird is most abundant during its migration in April where wooded parks, river valley systems and well-treed neighbourhoods seem to be overrun by the bird. Some creepers overwinter and can be found with flocks of chickadees.

HOUSE WREN
Troglodytes aedon
Troglodyte familier
smaller than sparrow-sized

ALTHOUGH NOT AS COMMON as some city birds, House Wrens have nevertheless adapted to the urban environment. A backyard with thick shubbery — especially if there's a nest box in a quiet corner — will often attract a pair.

House Wrens utilize cavities as nest sites but they readily accept nest boxes. Two broods are raised in a season and sometimes three. During the nesting period, they often change mates between broods. Evidence exists that male House Wrens sometimes maintain more than one mate at a time.

House Wrens sing with great energy throughout the day. They have a pleasant, rapid, chattering song which is easily recognized. They often scold, usually at nothing in particular.

This bird is the most common wren in our area. Its small size, brown upperparts and stubby tail identify it as a wren. Winter Wrens also inhabit the region but they spend the breeding season in habitats possessing more northern characteristics. Winter Wrens are smaller and they have definitive eyebrow stripes.

MARSH WREN

Cistothorus palustris
Troglodyte des marais
smaller than sparrow-sized

CATTAIL MARSHES ALONG THE LAKESHORE are home for this noisy bird. It prefers larger marshes, interspersed with areas of open water, such as those that can be found along our river systems. Any wren found in a cattail marsh in our region is likely this species. A similar-looking species, the Sedge Wren, does not frequent cattail habitats.

Although the bird tends to be elusive, you can still find it without difficulty. It sings almost constantly, its loud, bubbly, staccato-like song giving away its presence, sometimes even at night.

Marsh Wrens can occupy the same breeding area year after year. They are gregarious birds often nesting in loose colonies. The nests are balls of vegetation lashed onto the stems of cattails. An opening is left in the side of each nest as an entrance and the interior is lined with softer material. The female constructs the actual nest but the male builds several dummy nests nearby, the purpose of which is unclear. Five to six dull brown, spotted eggs are laid.

Marsh Wrens, though locally common, are absent from much of agricultural Ontario. As wetlands are drained, filled in and converted to other uses, Marsh Wren populations will decline as their habitats are lost.

75

GOLDEN-CROWNED KINGLET

Regulus satrapa
Roitelet à couronne dorée
smaller than sparrow-sized

KINGLETS ARE TINY, active, inconspicuous birds, olive-green and grey, with the centre of their crowns being orange bordered by yellow. They never seem to be still, frequently flicking their wings as they forage through the tree branches. The bird at times seems oblivious to human presence.

A more common breeding bird in northern Ontario than in southern areas, it can be abundant here during migration. Small numbers remain in winter where they can be found in conifers or mixed with flocks of chickadees.

Golden-crowned Kinglets are commonly found where mature stands of conifers are growing, especially where spruce is the most plentiful tree. The kinglets inhabit the upper portions of a dense conifer where they build their nests of moss, lichen and bark. Usually eight to nine very tiny eggs are laid.

The kinglet's voice is very high-pitched and can be easily missed.

WOOD THRUSH

Hylocichla mustelina
Grive des bois
robin-sized

THIS RETIRING THRUSH is a summer resident of woodlands with mature deciduous trees. It is best known for its clear, melodic bell-like song, heard mainly in early morning and in the evening. The thrush is often one of the earliest songsters, starting frequently before dawn.

The Wood Thrush can be told from other thrushes by its tawny or russet head which contrasts with its brown back and tail. Its white underparts are heavily spotted with large, black oval dots.

Most of its time is spent on or near the ground. Beetles, caterpillars and grasshoppers are among the variety of insects this bird finds amongst the woodland litter or gleans from the tree foliage.

The nest of a thrush is in a crotch or fixed upon a branch of a tree, sapling or shrub, frequently at a convenient height for viewing. The female incubates the three to four greenish-blue eggs, a colour not unlike that of robin eggs. Both parents feed the young and when the little birds are about twelve or thirteen days old, they leave the nest.

AMERICAN ROBIN

Turdus migratorius
Merle d' Amérique
robin-sized

THE AMERICAN ROBIN is a prime example of how well some birds can adapt to the human environment. In wild situations, the robin favours open broken woodland and forest clearings. Those open areas provide ideal sites for foraging. In the city, robins are equally at home, the manicured lawns replacing the open fields and forest openings as feeding areas. The bird is a natural inhabitant of back yards, parks and golf courses, where the ornamental trees and shrubs are much to its liking.

Although the robin is recognized as the harbinger of spring, some other species do return earlier. Sometimes robins can be found here in the winter. These are not mixed-up early migrants, but birds that are overwintering in a sheltered location where food has persisted during the cold months.

Not long after the snow has left the ground, robins can be seen running across the lawn in search of earthworms. As the season progresses, robins devour huge amounts of berries.

Although well adapted to the urban environment, local populations of this bird could be adversely affected by excessive use of pesticides in the gardens or parks.

GRAY CATBIRD
Dumetella carolinensis
Moqueur chat
smaller than robin-sized

A GRAY CATBIRD is easily identified. It is mostly slate-grey, with a black cap and a patch of chestnut under the tail. An inhabitant of hedges and shrubs in city gardens and fields, its attractive song is often heard. The song is a series of pleasant musical phrases, sometimes discordant, and other times imitating the songs of other birds. As well, a soft cat-like mewing, which is unmistakable, is often used.

Most of the catbird's diet is comprised of insects like crickets, grasshoppers or June beetles, making it a valuable asset to the garden. Later in the summer, it eats many kinds of wild berries such as elderberry or wild grape.

The bulky nest is constructed with a combination of twigs, grass and weed stems and the interior is lined with fine rootlets and shreds of bark. It is usually between one and three metres above the ground. The three to five unmarked, greenish-blue eggs are incubated by the female.

Gray Catbirds can be abundant in retired farmland and pasture where hawthorns, old apple trees and other shrubbery bushes are common. Homeowners who have an acre or two in old farm areas are almost sure to have this vocal bird establishing its territory each spring.

BROWN THRASHER

Toxostoma rufum
Moqueur roux
robin-sized

THRASHERS OCCUPY SIMILAR HABITATS to Gray Catbirds but they tend to show a preference for dense, thorny bushes. Retired, marginal farmland with many hawthorns are good places to look for this bird. Unlike the Catbird, the Brown Thrasher shuns human habitation, as it is a shyer bird.

The nest of a thrasher is built low, sometimes even on the ground, in dense thickets and shrubbery. The nest, containing four to five bluish-white eggs covered with small brown dots, is loosely constructed of twigs, bark and grass, and lined with fine rootlets.

Brown Thrashers feed most of the time on the ground, foraging among the fallen leaves and plant litter underneath shrubs and trees. They seldom scratch the ground with their feet but use their bills to toss the leaves aside in the search for grubs and beetles. They will jump from the ground to catch flying insects and later in the season, when berries are ripe, they eagerly devour the fruit.

A loud songster, the thrasher perches atop a bush or tree to sing, making it easy to spot. The song is a series of musical notes with many of the phrases repeated in pairs.

BOHEMIAN WAXWING

Bombycilla garrulus
Jaseur boréal
larger than sparrow-sized

THESE HANDSOME VISITORS can be found in the Capital region only in winter. Most of the time they feed in flocks on the berries of various trees and shrubs, particularly mountain ash. Their wheezy chattering call readily identifies them as waxwings as they move from tree to tree to gorge themselves on the winter fruit. Some winters when the berry crop is very poor, the bird may be very scarce indeed. Normally, due to the large number of berry-producing trees and shrubs, the Arboretum of the Central Experimental Farm is an excellent location to see the species.

Unlike the closely related Cedar Waxwing, there is only scanty evidence of this bird's breeding in Ontario. Bohemians can be told from Cedar Waxwings by their larger size, more greyish appearance, warm chestnut under the tail and the white and yellow "wax-like" colouration on the wing.

CEDAR WAXWING
Bombycilla cedrorum
Jaseur des cèdres
larger than sparrow-sized

THIS SPECIES, at first glance, is similar to the Bohemian Waxwing, only not as large. Unlike its relative, the Cedar Waxwing can be found throughout most of Ontario and is a common breeding bird.

The Cedar Waxwing uses a variety of habitats; consequently, the bird is one of the most widespread breeding birds in the province, and can be found in residential areas and open woodlands.

It is one of the later nesting birds, as the usual nesting period is from late June through August. The three to five eggs are pale bluish-grey with dots of black and are laid in a bulky nest, located in a tree or shrub.

Cedar Waxwings devour many insects in summer and are, because of this, quite beneficial. However, they gorge themselves on berries, and their fondness for cherries may bring on the wrath of fruit growers.

EUROPEAN STARLING

Sturnus vulgaris
Étourneau sansonnet
smaller than robin-sized

THE EUROPEAN STARLING is with us year round. Introduced to New York in 1890 from Europe, starlings have shown remarkable ability to adapt to surroundings, spreading rapidly from one end of the continent to the other.

The bird nests in tree cavities, crevices or openings in buildings and old fence posts. In natural situations, the aggressive starling often displaces native birds from their nest sites.

Starlings can roost in huge numbers, upsetting more than one neighbourhood with the noise and mess as the trees are occupied for roosting.

Starlings also do immense good, feeding on weed seeds or insects and grubs on lawns or city parks. No doubt, they will also visit your bird feeder.

A terrific mimic, starlings incorporate parts of other bird songs into their own as well as a variety of squeaks and whistles from the neighbourhood. You can often tell when some of the spring bird species have arrived back in your neighborhood by listening for starlings mimicking their calls. Killdeers and Red-tailed Hawks are among their favorite song imitations.

WARBLING VIREO
Vireo gilvus
Viréo mélodieux
sparrow-sized

THIS DRAB, PALE GREY VIREO has no obvious field marks but does it sing! A treetop bird, the male sings continuously, filling the air with its song from its arrival in spring until late summer. Even on the hottest, most humid days its flowing warble can be heard.

An open woodland bird, it is at home in the mature shady trees of our parks and neighbourhoods. Where such trees exist, the Warbling Vireo is usually present.

The nest is a well made cup suspended from a fork of a twig high up in the tree. Three to five eggs are laid which are incubated by both sexes. The nest is difficult to find as it is often obscured by the leaves in the tree-top.

Warbling Vireos forage for insects in the tree canopy. Caterpillars, insect larvae, and other assorted bugs make up their diet.

RED-EYED VIREO
Vireo olivaceus
Viréo aux yeux rouges
sparrow-sized

VIREOS ARE SMALL PLAIN WOODLAND BIRDS that lack any conspicuous plumage pattern. They are dull greenish-olive on the upperparts. The term vireo is derived from Latin, referring to this dull colouration.

Although and hard to distinguish in the field, the vireo is one of our most common songbirds. Scarcely a city park, ravine or wooded neighbourhood is without Red-eyed Vireos. The bird is a persistent singer, delivering its song tirelessly throughout the day, even on the hottest afternoon when other birds are silent.

This vireo primarily inhabits broad-leaved trees and tall shrubbery. Here in a slow, deliberate pattern it forages among the leaves for insects. The dull colouration makes it difficult to see, but once you are familiar with its song you will detect it in woodlots everywhere.

Usually the nest is constructed at about eye level. It is a well made cup suspended by its edge in the fork of a branch. The nests persist throughout the winter, and many empty nests found in winter belong to this species.

Voracious eaters of insects, Red-eyed Vireos are highly beneficial to humans.

YELLOW WARBLER
Dendroica petechia
Paruline jaune
smaller than sparrow-sized

THIS BRIGHT COLOURFUL SONGSTER is often called a wild canary and is the most likely warbler to be seen in the city by the casual observer. Easily identified by sight, the male has reddish breast streaks that can be seen at close distance over its yellow body. The streaks are faint or absent in the female and overall, she is a paler colour. Watch for the brighter yellow tail patches in both sexes.

Most Yellow Warblers return to southern Ontario in early May but some individuals can be seen in late April. The males start singing as soon as they arrive, to establish their territories. It is then that the birds are easy to spot, before all the trees and shrubs are in full leaf. They live in the shrubbery of gardens, along the edges of ponds and streams, but they avoid dense wooded areas.

The nest is fastened to the fork of a branch and is made of grasses and other material.

Yellow Warblers are one of our earliest warblers to arrive in spring but by the end of August most have already begun their migration south.

YELLOW-RUMPED WARBLER

Dendroica coronata
Paruline à croupion jaune
smaller than sparrow-sized

OF ALL THE COLOURFUL SONGBIRDS that appear in spring in our gardens and parks, the Yellow-rumped Warbler is one of the most numerous. It is the earliest warbler to arrive, usually in late April, and is the last warbler species to depart in autumn.

The bright yellow rump combined with a yellow patch on each side of the breast distinguishes this species from other warblers.

The Yellow-rumped Warbler is widespread as a breeding bird in Ontario, preferring coniferous woodlands. It adapts readily to areas disturbed by power lines, fire or logging, as it likes to inhabit the edges of forest openings.

The nest is built in a coniferous tree and made of twigs and grass. The inside is lined with feathers and hair. The female incubates the four to five white eggs with grey and brown specks.

Yellow-rumped Warblers have one of the most extensive distribution ranges in Canada, being found from the Atlantic coast to the Pacific and to the Mackenzie River Delta: wherever coniferous habitat is found.

BLACK-AND-WHITE WARBLER

Mniotilta varia
Paruline noir et blanc
smaller than sparrow-sized

THIS BIRD IS BOLDLY STRIPED in black and white, except on the belly which is pure white. It creeps along branches and trunks of trees, a habit which distinguishes it from other warblers.

Widely distributed in Ontario, the Black-and-white Warbler is among the four or five early species of warbler to return in the spring. It is a quiet bird and unlike some other warbler species it can be inconspicuous. Its song is a high-pitched, thin, *weesee, weesee, weesee, weesee*.

Like so many other species in spring, the city parks and natural areas are excellent places to see this species, as are older neighbourhoods with lots of trees; although during migration, an area can be alive with birds one day and virtually empty the next. Vincent Massey Park and Britannia are possibly the best places in Ottawa for seeing warblers during migration.

This bird breeds in deciduous or mixed woodlands, often in moist areas like cedar swamps, which are especially attractive. The nest is built on the ground, often at the base of a tree or stump. Five eggs are laid in the well concealed nest.

AMERICAN REDSTART

Setophaga ruticilla
Paruline flamboyante
smaller than sparrow-sized

THE SHOWY COLOURS AND CONSTANT ACTIVITY of this flashy warbler make it immediately recognizable, a spectacular "butterfly" of the bird world. Rarely still, the Redstart flits from bush to bush, snatching up insects from the twigs and leaves and darting out to catch insects on the wing.

Redstarts are inhabitants of the deciduous woodlands in the summer, frequenting the shrubby understory. They can often be seen in back yards during migration. These birds are particularly common in cottage areas, where the re-generating second growth woodlands are much to their preference.

The startling orange and black colour combination and white underparts of the male make it unmistakable. The female has yellow patches in place of orange and a greyish head blending into olive on the back. The male does not acquire the black adult plumage until its second year.

The well built nest of this bird is settled in an upright crotch of a young tree or in a large shrub. The cup-shaped nest likely contains four whitish, brown-spotted eggs which are incubated by the female. Redstarts have a high-pitched variable song. As soon as you've learned one song, a different rendition is heard, making this a difficult bird to identify by sound alone.

OVENBIRD

Seiurus aurocapillus
Paruline couronnée
sparrow-sized

THIS IS A BIRD THAT you will hear more often than see. Its loud, repetitive song, *teacher-teacher-teacher*, is easily recognized and for a few days in May, the song reverberates throughout our wooded river valleys and parks. After this brief interlude, you will rarely find the Ovenbird in urban areas except in relatively undisturbed woodlots or in wilder parks like the Gatineau.

The Ovenbird is typically an inhabitant of older deciduous and mixed forests, where the tree canopy obscures the sky and there is little shrubby understory but a lot of leaf litter.

This bird is usually seen walking on the ground or on a low branch. It is a large warbler but its colour allows it to blend into the forest floor. It will rarely flush in the woods unless an intruder is virtually upon it.

The nest is built on the ground, often in a more open area of the forest. It is constructed in the form of an arch with the opening in front. The dead-leaf roof sheds the rain and conceals the nest. The overall shape of the nest is like an oven, for which the bird is named. As a ground nester, it is subject to much predation from snakes, squirrels and skunks and other animals that forage on the forest floor.

COMMON YELLOWTHROAT

Geothlypis trichas
Paruline masquée
smaller than sparrow-sized

YELLOWTHROATS occupy a variety of habitats from the edges of streams, to bogs, low bushes and thickets in moist areas, but in our region they are most often found in the cattail marshes of the river valleys surrounding the city.

The song of the Yellowthroat is a loud *whitchita, whitchita, whitchita, whit,* and can be identified without too much difficulty. In breeding season, the male can be seen singing from a prominent perch within the marsh. Usually the birds carry out most of their activities in the lower levels of vegetation; consequently, they can be annoyingly difficult to see. Yellowthroats are extremely active birds, almost wren-like in their energy.

The nest is constructed on the ground or slightly above it. Made of weed stalks, grasses, sedges and other material, it seems rather bulky. Four eggs are laid and incubated by the female for about twelve days. When the young hatch, both parents can be seen carrying food to the nest.

ROSE-BREASTED GROSBEAK

Pheucticus ludovicianus
Cardinal à poitrine rose
smaller than robin-sized

THIS BIRD IS A COMMON SUMMER RESIDENT around Ottawa wherever second growth and mature broad-leaved woodlands are found. You can find the bird along the edges of woodlands, pastures, borders of streams and in the wooded parks, ravines, and treed areas of the city.

The grosbeak sings a continuous melodic song, similar to that of a robin, but more forceful, rapid and rich in tone. Because of its constant song, we can easily spot the male. Its conspicuous rose breast contrasts sharply with its white underparts and black head, throat and back. Although the male provides us with a glimpse of tropical-like beauty, the female is much duller, being a dark buffy brown with white brown-streaked underparts.

Male grosbeaks sometimes select the nest site and may help the female construct the nest, which is located in tall shrubbery or small trees. While the nests are usually at a relatively low height, they can be constructed as high as eight to fifteen metres up, in which case they are always in deciduous trees.

Rose-breasted Grosbeaks forage in trees, feeding on insects, buds, blossoms and fruit.

INDIGO BUNTING

Passerina cyanea
Passerin indigo
sparrow-sized

INDIGO BUNTINGS are a relatively common summer resident of the pastures and shrubby fields within our region, singing conspicuously from high perches such as utility wires or exposed branches. This behaviour constitutes an aggressive defense of their territories against other males. The species prefers an area with bushy ground cover for nest sites, and trees along the woodland edge for singing; therefore, they are common along roadsides, and utility rights-of-way.

The name "bunting" is of unknown origin. The species' scientific name, *cyanea*, means dark blue, an excellent description for the male Indigo Bunting. It is one of the most handsome songbirds in Ontario.

The nest is a cup-like structure not far from the ground within a clump of raspberry bushes or equally impenetrable bushes. The female incubates her three or four blue-white eggs for twelve to thirteen days. About ten days after hatching the young leave the nest.

Buntings forage in trees, shrubbery or on the ground where they eat a variety of food, from grasshoppers and beetles to the seeds of dandelion, thistle, aster and goldenrod.

The breeding range for Indigo Buntings in Ontario is restricted to regions of deciduous or mixed wood forest but they are not found in predominantly coniferous forests. In winter, these birds migrate to the Caribbean and Central America.

AMERICAN TREE SPARROW

Spizella arborea
Bruant hudsonien
sparrow-sized

WHEN THE WINDS OF AUTUMN remind us that winter is just around the corner, Tree Sparrows begin to make their appearance, en route from the far north. In small flocks, they move about in the backyard shrubbery or roadside wooded edges, rummaging for seeds.

A Tree Sparrow is distinguished by the brown blotch in the middle of its clear, grey breast. Two white wing-bars are prominent, as is the rusty brown cap.

The bird nests along the tree-line areas of Ontario where there are shrubs, like willow or dwarf birch. The nest can be on the ground or placed in one of the low shrubs.

Watch for the American Tree Sparrow in the winter at your feeder, or in weedy fields or roadside areas that provide a good supply of seed.

CHIPPING SPARROW

Spizella passerina
Bruant familier
smaller than sparrow-sized

THE CHIPPING SPARROW can be found in the summer in the openings and edges of woodlands, near scattered trees, and in orchards, gardens, parks and cemeteries. Because of its preference for grassy areas and scattered trees, it has adapted well to the human environment: in fact, it is probably the most domesticated of our native sparrows. The species is abundant in urban areas and is often one of the first species in a new subdivision area.

The bird gets its name from its song of chipping call notes.

The small, compact nest is often located at moderate height in an evergreen. The female builds it, using grass and weed stems, and lines it with finer material such as hair. She lays four light blue, spotted eggs and incubates them for about eleven to thirteen days.

The Chipping Sparrow eats large amounts of weed seeds found in our lawns including crabgrass and dandelion, among others. Insects are also eaten.

FIELD SPARROW
Spizella pusilla
Bruant des champs
sparrow-sized

THE FIELD SPARROW has an unstreaked breast, pink bill, rusty cap, and rusty upperparts. The song of this bird is quite pleasing and distinctive.

Abandoned farmlands, overgrown pastures and similar areas are typical habitats for this bird. In more rural areas, deserted farmland often provides ideal habitat. Conversely, extensive cultivation of farmland has eliminated much habitat suitable for the bird.

The nest of the Field Sparrow can be found on or near the ground either in the grass or small shrubs. The male defends his territory against other males by flying to various trees and shrubs, announcing his presence with his sweet, whistled song.

Top: Field Sparrow
Middle: Song Sparrow
Bottom: Savannah Sparrow

SAVANNAH SPARROW

Passerculus sandwichensis
Bruant des prés
smaller than sparrow-sized

AN INHABITANT of open grasslands, meadows, pastures and hayfields the Savannah Sparrow is one of the most widely distributed birds in Canada. You can find it in the Arctic as well as in the hydro rights-of-way behind your house.

A nondescript streaked sparrow, it has a yellow line above the eye. The bird is a persistent singer, and can often be seen singing from perches on fences, wires, bushes or tall plants.

The nest is well concealed on the ground in a natural hollow, or in one made by the bird. Four to six whitish eggs, variously splashed with brown, are laid. Both parents incubate the eggs.

SONG SPARROW

Melospiza melodia
Bruant chanteur
sparrow-sized

AN EARLY ARRIVAL IN SPRING, the Song Sparrow can begin nesting in mid-April. This species is common in thickets, along the margins of ponds, streams and rivers. It is a resident of treed neighbourhoods and it can be a nesting species in your backyard.

Most nests are built on the ground, especially those built early in the season. In southern Ontario, two or three broods can be produced in a season, with three to five eggs in each brood.

The Song Sparrow's food supply is comprised mostly of insects in summer but as the season progresses, it also includes the fruit of many shrubs. Song Sparrows will also visit bird feeders.

WHITE-THROATED SPARROW

Zonotrichia albicollis
Bruant à gorge blanche
sparrow-sized

THIS CHUNKY SPARROW with its striped head and well defined white throat patch is an abundant migrant through our region. Ravines, brush piles, back yard shrubbery and wooded parks can be virtually alive with this species in spring. Its song, variously described as *Sam Peabody, Peabody, Peabody* or *I-love-Canada, Canada, Canada* vibrates through wooded residential areas, adding to the festive atmosphere of spring.

White-throated Sparrows are quite widespread. Those of us who have spent any time in cottage country or in places like Algonquin Park are as familiar with this species as a symbol of Ontario's wild as we are of the Common Loon. In the Capital region, this bird is common in Gatineau Park.

A resident of bushy openings, cutover areas or the edges of mixed wood forest, whitethroats build their nests on or near the ground in thickets or beneath shrubs. Generally, four eggs are laid.

Occasionally, an individual of this species may remain in our region during the winter months.

DARK-EYED JUNCO

Junco hyemalis
Junco ardoisé
sparrow-sized

ADULT JUNCOS are easily recognized sparrows: the distinctive grey hood, sharply separated from the white underparts and white outer tail feathers are the diagnostic features of this bird.

A very common migrant in our region in April and late fall, it may remain during winter and show up at our feeders. In the nesting season, the Junco is primarily an inhabitant of the mixed forest area on the Canadian Shield. It does not inhabit the deep forest but prefers the woodland edges and forest openings. The bird appears to like burned-over areas. Its trilling song is commonplace throughout the lake and cottage country of the province.

The Junco's nest is usually on the ground in a forest opening, well hidden in the shelter of a tree or stump. Four to five eggs are laid in the cup-shaped nest. Young juncos leave the nest when about thirteen days old.

During migration, watch for the species in your backyard, wooded river valleys or ravines and similar wooded habitats.

BOBOLINK
Dolichonyx oryzivorus
Goglu
smaller than robin-sized

BOBOLINKS MIGRATE NORTHWARD each spring from southern Brazil and northern Argentina to the fields of southern Canada. The males arrive several days ahead of the females filling the air with their tinkling, bubbling songs as they engage in aerial displays. Their migration flight is the longest undertaken by a member of the blackbird family.

The males are strikingly handsome, coloured in black, white and yellowish-buff. The females, on the other hand, are somewhat nondescript, an excellent adaption for a bird that nests on the ground.

Bobolinks are residents of open fields containing taller grasses, clover and wildflowers, or agricultural fields containing alfalfa. The bird is common in agricultural Ontario and can be seen from May to August in the open fields surrounding the city.

In summer, this bird eats large quantities of beetles, grasshoppers and other insects as well as grass seeds. It also eats rice: in the early part of this century, the Bobolink was sought out and killed for the damage it inflicted on rice crops in the southern United States.

RED-WINGED BLACKBIRD

Agelaius phoeniceus
Carouge à épaulettes
smaller than robin-sized

THIS SUMMER BIRD has a *konk-a-ree* song, and a distinctive appearance. The males are hard to misidentify, as they perch on the cattails of marshes or water edges, displaying bright red wing patches.

The Red-wing often nests in loose colonies. Its rough, grass nest is built over water on two or more cattail stalks. Here the female incubates her four eggs, while the male keeps watch to protect his territory from other Red-wings. The colonies can be noisy, as the males will call frequently to resolve territorial disputes.

Although primarily a resident of marshes, Red-wings have adapted to life in pastures and roadsides. They roost in large numbers, and huge flocks can be seen blackening the sky as the birds leave their roosting area. After the nesting period, the birds can be found everywhere. They feed on waste grain in the agricultural fields but sometimes cause damage to standing corn.

Any wetland around the city will contain these birds during the breeding season. They often visit bird feeders.

EASTERN MEADOWLARK

Sturnella magna
Sturnelle des prés
robin-sized

EASTERN MEADOWLARKS are birds of open, grassy areas and occupy the fields, meadows and pastures surrounding our region. Within the city itself, weedy areas, utility rights-of-way and similar open spaces often contain a pair or two. Despite the common name, the bird is not a lark but a member of the blackbird family.

The clear song of this brownish bird, with its rich lemon-yellow breast, is rendered from fence posts, utility poles and wires.

The males return first in April, followed by females a week or so later. Resident males then begin to sing more, proclaiming their territory. Some males may have more than one mate.

The nest of the Meadowlark, concealed in the grass, often has a domed-shaped roof. The five eggs are incubated by the female but both parents feed the young.

Eastern Meadowlarks are voracious eaters of a variety of insects.

COMMON GRACKLE
Quiscalus quiscula
Quiscale bronzé
robin-sized

COMMON GRACKLES appear early in spring. Very common in our region, they tend to gather in flocks and frequently mix with Red-winged Blackbirds, Starlings and Brown-headed Cowbirds. They appear black with a long, wedge-shaped tail but a close look at one of these birds will reveal a surprisingly handsome iridescent plumage of blue, purple and bronze.

Easily satisfied in their habitat requirements, grackles can be found on lawns and golf courses, or in marshes, parks or wet woodlands. The broad habitat use displayed by the species is also reflected in its wide-ranging diet. Weed seeds, waste grain, insects, garbage and young nestlings and eggs of other species keep the bird well fed.

Highly gregarious, the species can roost at night in huge numbers. Although individual nests are found, grackles nest in small colonies as well. The bulky nests of this bird are built of sticks and weeds and are plastered together with mud. Grackles frequently select conifers for nesting but as the habitat description suggests, the nest may be constructed in a variety of places. The four to six eggs are incubated by the female.

BROWN-HEADED COWBIRD

Molothrus ater
Vacher à tête brune
sparrow-sized

THE COWBIRD IS WIDESPREAD in agricultural and residential areas, where it forages for insects and weed seeds in open grassy areas or cultivated fields. The name is derived from its association with cattle, as the bird feeds on the insects kicked up by these animals.

Famous or notorious, depending on your point of view, for their parasitic habits, cowbirds build no nests. Instead, the females lay their eggs in the nests of other small birds like Yellow Warblers or Chipping Sparrows. There is some evidence that indicates a female cowbird can lay up to ten or twelve eggs each season, each in the nest of a different bird.

The host bird may push the cowbird egg from the nest but most often, the egg is incubated along with its own. Cowbirds hatch first and develop rapidly. The persistent begging of the young bird, as well as its fast growth and aggressive behaviour mean the host's young are deprived of food and may eventually die. Sometimes the young cowbird will push the other young from the nest. The host bird will continue to feed the young cowbird, oblivious to the fact that it is a different species.

NORTHERN ORIOLE

Icterus galbula
Oriole du Nord
robin-sized

THE NORTHERN ORIOLE is one of the most striking birds to be seen in Canada. The vivid orange underparts, contrasting with the solid black head, leave little room for misidentification. The female is less vividly coloured, being olive above and a dull yellow-orange below.

A resident of the upper parts of tall deciduous trees, it is often obscured from our sight by the foliage, but its loud, distinct, melodious song gives the bird away. The male is a frequent singer in May but once paired, he sings much less frequently. This bird can be easily imitated by even the worst whistler, and will actually come down to scold at and sing with a human intruder.

The nest is not too difficult to find as it is an obvious bag-like structure suspended from a tree branch, carefully woven with various plant fibres. The entrance to this hanging structure is from the top. In autumn, when the leaves have fallen, the used nests are easily sighted.

Northern Orioles consume a variety of insects and are one of the few bird species that consume tent caterpillars.

Look for the bird along woodland edges, open wooded roadsides, parks and neighbourhoods where tall shady trees are found.

PINE GROSBEAK

Pinicola enucleator

Dur-bec des pins

smaller than robin-sized

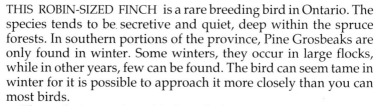

THIS ROBIN-SIZED FINCH is a rare breeding bird in Ontario. The species tends to be secretive and quiet, deep within the spruce forests. In southern portions of the province, Pine Grosbeaks are only found in winter. Some winters, they occur in large flocks, while in other years, few can be found. The bird can seem tame in winter for it is possible to approach it more closely than you can most birds.

The male is mainly reddish with dark wings and white bars while the female is more silvery grey with yellowish tinges.

The species tends to favour the soft fruits left on bushes and trees during the winter. Mountain ash berries and crabapples are among their favorites. They will also feed on maple and ash seeds as well as the seeds of conifers.

Areas having large numbers of ornamental trees and bushes or wild berry-bearing shrubs are good places to look for the species. The Arboretum is particularly reliable.

HOUSE FINCH
Carpodacus mexicanus
Roselin familier
smaller than sparrow-sized

THE HOUSE FINCH is a recent arrival to southern Ontario. Breeding evidence for the bird was not obtained in Ontario until 1978 but since that time, the population has expanded rapidly.

It is now a common species in southern Ontario but especially in urban centres where a variety of nesting sites are provided.

It nests in ornamental bushes and shrubs, evergreens, buildings or bird boxes. Four to five speckled, blue-white eggs are laid in the nest, usually located about two to three metres along the ground. Two broods are raised during the long nesting season.

The male House Finch is a conspicuous songster, its bright red crown, chest and rump and striped flanks distinguish it from the Purple Finch.

The House Finch is very adaptable to man, a characteristic shared with the House Sparrow. In southwestern North America, the species occupies a niche similar to the House Sparrow and as it spreads in our area, it occupies the same habitat.

COMMON REDPOLL
Carduelis flammea
Sizerin flammé
smaller than sparrow-sized

ANOTHER WINTER FINCH, the Common Redpoll breeds only in far northern latitudes such as the barrenlands and shrub-tundra areas of the Hudson Bay lowlands. In winter, the species may be found here in large numbers one year, then there may be none the next year. When present, the immense flocks move around restlessly over weedy fields, devouring the seed heads projecting above the snow. Redpolls are also fond of birch and alder seeds.

Sometimes a Hoary Redpoll may be mixed in with a flock of Common Redpolls. This species may appear lighter and slightly larger than a Common Redpoll but the only reliable field mark is the whitish unstreaked rump of the Hoary Redpoll.

The Common Redpoll may be seen individually at bird feeders, which it visits for millet and the small variety of sunflower seeds. Whole groups of redpolls can be attracted to feeders containing the more expensive niger seed.

On the tundra breeding grounds, redpolls construct their nests in small shrubs, one of the few far northern nesting birds to build nests above the ground.

PINE SISKIN

Carduelis pinus
Chardonneret des pins
smaller than sparrow-sized

THIS SMALL, HEAVILY STREAKED brownish bird can be a delight to have around the bird feeder. The yellow in its wings and tail is not very noticeable when it perches but is immediately visible when it takes flight.

Pine Siskins are erratic in their presence in southern Ontario. They can be abundant one year and virtually absent in the same area the next. In years of high abundance, a few siskins may remain to nest overwinter. The species tends to be gregarious and even during the nesting season, they can be found in small flocks.

This bird prefers habitats of mixed coniferous and deciduous trees but it can use ornamental bushes and shady tree areas for nesting. The nest, a cup made of fine twigs and rootlets, is usually built in a conifer. Three to five pale blue eggs are laid in very early spring.

Pine Siskins eat the seeds of conifers, birch and dandelions as well as small buds and insects.

AMERICAN GOLDFINCH

Carduelis tristis
Chardonneret jaune
smaller than sparrow-sized

THE "WILD CANARY" of the countryside, the American Goldfinch is common throughout southern Ontario. The bright yellow colouration of the male with its black cap, wings and tail, is unmistakable. The female is more drab: brownish olive, tinged with yellow and with no black cap. The adults in winter are mainly brownish olive.

Goldfinches are often seen in flocks. Their obvious undulating flight is a characteristic field mark.

These birds nest later than most: they do not commence nesting until well into July. It is believed that this timing is an adaptation to coincide with the growth of summer seeds, such as those of the thistle, which the young goldfinches are fed. Old pastures with small shrubs and hawthorns are the best places to find this bird.

Goldfinches can be common in residential areas where they visit gardens to feed on the seeds of cosmos and zinnias among others. They are also visitors to the feeder in some winters, when they enjoy the smallest variety of sunflower, and niger seed.

EVENING GROSBEAK

Coccothraustes vespertinus
Gros-bec errant
robin-sized

COMMONLY SEEN IN WINTER, Evening Grosbeaks will feed on maple and ash keys, small crabapples, or mountain ash berries. They are most famous for descending upon bird feeders in urban areas where they gorge themselves on sunflower seeds. Their arrival at the bird feeder can be exciting, as they are resplendent against the snow. Depending upon the depth of your pocketbook, their continued presence at the feeder may start to wear a little thin, given their ravenous appetite.

The plumage of the male is an elegant black, white and yellow, while the adult female is mostly greyish, tinged with greenish yellow. It is a plump bird with a distinctive, undulating flight pattern. The large white wing patches are very noticeable in flight.

The breeding habitat of the Evening Grosbeak is primarily in the coniferous and mixed wood areas of the province where it can nest in either a coniferous or deciduous tree.

The bird wanders widely after nesting. In the Capital region it is most easily located during the winter months, but the species may be seen any time in areas like Gatineau Park.

HOUSE SPARROW

Passer domesticus
Moineau domestique
sparrow-sized

THE COMMON HOUSE SPARROW is a stocky, noisy bird with a black throat and bib, and chestnut markings. The female is duller and unmarked, and can be easily confused with other species of sparrow.

Sparrows are often seen in flocks, as most of us who operate feeding stations will readily agree. They survive with no difficulty wherever there is human settlement, from the city core to the rural farm. Not native to North America, the bird rapidly adapted to the New World after its introduction in the middle of the nineteenth century. In fact, it has obtained the status of pest in many areas.

House Sparrows will nest anywhere and will frequently take over nest boxes set out to attract other species. About five eggs are laid. They are incubated generally by the female, although she is sometimes assisted by the male.

The song is a simple series of chirps, repeated over and over.

Despite their being labelled as pests, House Sparrows are beneficial to mankind, as they help clean up human garbage.

ATTRACTING BIRDS

GETTING STARTED at birdwatching need not cost a lot of money. Many people derive a great deal of pleasure by simply putting out household scraps for birds on a homemade feeder, close enough to the window that birds can be seen as they come and go.

It is certainly not necessary to be able to identify all the birds at the feeder to be able to enjoy them, but there is a great sense of satisfaction in being able to tell one species from another. Human nature being what it is, we tend to want to learn.

Most people interested in watching birds use binoculars, as this allows them to identify key characteristics such as plumage, leg colour, and bill shape. Binoculars also allow the user to watch the more timid birds that normally stay at a distance, or remain in the cover of bushes and trees, and they allow us to study birds' behaviour. Small details help to build the overall picture of a bird, which helps to identify the species.

Buying binoculars is perhaps the biggest financial outlay the birdwatcher will make, but it is not necessary to spend a great deal

An attractive back yard offers many birdwatching opportunities.

of money as there are many inexpensive but good models. Buying binoculars can be confusing, and much has been written about how to choose a pair. The best advice is to ask a birdwatcher or to talk to someone at a local nature centre. Remember that no one pair will be perfect for every situation — watching birds in woodland requires binoculars with a wide field of view but a reasonably low magnification (8X would be ideal), whereas watching shorebirds in an estuary would require a higher magnification, and a telescope would then be useful. Binoculars tend to get heavy around the neck, and it is a good idea to keep this in mind when selecting the right pair. A wider neck strap certainly helps, but if you have a choice, you will not regret going for the lightest pair that seems to be right for you.

Aside from binoculars, the only other piece of equipment needed is a book that will enable you to identify the birds you see. Armed with a pair of binoculars and a good field guide, you will find a whole new world opening up for you as you take advantage of the many excellent birdwatching sites in and around the city, or enjoy your own back yard birds more.

Soon, you will be taking your binoculars with you on a hike or as you take the dog for a walk in the park — the opportunities for their use are endless.

Birds are easily viewed in their natural habitat through binoculars.

BIRD FEEDERS

Why bother with a bird feeder in your back yard? The great advantage is that by feeding birds on a regular basis, they learn to come to that spot every day and as more birds learn, the numbers of species and individuals increase. Your back yard can become your own bird sanctuary.

Feeders also provide advantages for birds. They are used much more frequently when natural food sources are less abundant—particularly in the winter months. When the weather gets colder, the birds using the neighbourhood feeders may rely on this food source for survival. Late autumn is a good time to establish feeders, as this is when birds are setting up their winter territories.

Once feeding is started, it should be maintained throughout the winter and particularly during the colder weather. A break in the normal routine could well mean that the birds you have so carefully attracted will move on or may not survive. Try feeding the birds at the same time each day and you will notice how they quickly adjust to a daily routine. Early morning is best. Better still, provide sufficient food to last two or three days.

There may only be a few birds at the feeder at any one time, but this does not necessarily mean that only a few birds are using the feeder. It can be difficult to recognize individuals, but by banding and watching them as they come back to feeders, it has been shown that birds use feeders for only short periods during the day. Any one feeder may be visited by many individuals throughout the

Blue Jays feeding at a tray feeder.

Black-capped Chickadees at a seed dispenser.

daylight hours as they forage through the neighbourhood. This is normal, particularly in the winter when they must range over a much wider area to find the variety of foods they need to sustain themselves.

When you place a feeder in the garden, don't expect the birds to find it immediately. It often takes a few weeks for numbers to build up, so persevere and be patient.

It is best to position the feeder some distance from the house, as the birds will be wary if they see movement. Find a site that is likely to be attractive to birds: immediately adjacent to dense trees or bushes for instance, rather than in the centre of the lawn. Immediate escape cover is as important as the food itself. Small birds are innately aware of the danger of avian predators such as hawks, and will soon take a liking to a feeder that offers safety as well as good fare.

Bear in mind also that cats can be a real threat, so make it difficult for them by ensuring that the birds have a chance to see them. Avoid positioning your feeder right beside a suitable hiding place, such as a low bush, and make sure that it is high enough to be out of reach of the agile cat — which can leap as high as two metres. A large circle of page wire under the feeder will soon dissuade the neighbour's Tabby.

There are countless designs for bird feeders, but essentially they all do exactly the same job: they dispense food for birds in a convenient and hygienic manner. Depending on the type of birds one wishes to attract, there are four basic designs:

- hanging seed dispensers
- tray feeders for mixed bird foods
- suet feeders
- hummingbird feeders

Hanging Seed Dispensers

These come in many different designs, but if you bear a few points in mind it is easy to select the right one.

The feeder should be large enough to hold a good supply of seeds; otherwise, you will be forever refilling it. The ease with which the feeder can be filled is also important. Birds will eat most during the coldest periods, so you'll need a feeder that is easy to open and close on a cold day when you're wearing gloves.

All feeders should be cleaned regularly so they should be easy to take apart. The seed should be protected from the rain and snow. Clear plastic seed containers are the best — they clean easily, are reasonably strong, allow you to see when they need refilling, and allow the birds to see what is inside them.

There are many commercial seed mixtures available for hang-

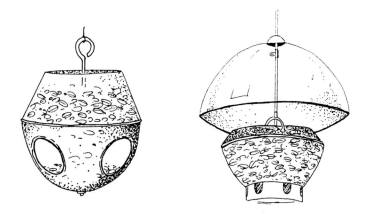

LEFT: A large seed dispenser that holds more food and has larger openings to allow bigger birds to use it.
RIGHT: A seed hopper with a plastic dome that keeps off squirrels and larger birds. It has good seed capability and is ideal for small birds.

ing feeders, but a surprising number of birds seem to prefer sunflower seeds. It is a favorite food of Evening Grosbeaks, Blue Jays, Black-capped Chickadees and Northern Cardinals, among others. There are two types of sunflower seeds, the larger, striped variety and the smaller black one. Many winter finches prefer the latter.

Cracked corn is enjoyed by many species and is inexpensive compared to other foods. The "wild bird seed" mixtures will attract a number of birds, mainly House Sparrows. If you really want to please a Blue Jay, put out peanuts.

Tray Feeders

This type of feeder can be designed to attract many different types of birds, from seed eaters to those that forage on the ground. Some tray feeders have a hopper, with the tray immediately below to catch the seed and provide a feeding area. These work well, but have some disadvantages. There is never enough room for all the birds to feed without overcrowding, and so the more dominant species and individuals tend to drive others away. It is also quite difficult to see the birds at the feeder. The more timid ones tend to feed on the side furthest from your sight — a problem which can be overcome if you arrange to have only one outlet.

Perhaps the best types of tray feeders are those that are nothing more than a large tray, onto which seed and other scraps are spread. It should have a lip to stop too much food from spilling or

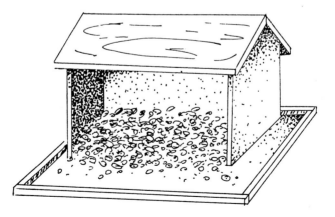

A tray-type feeder with a hopper that has a see-through side for easy checking of food levels.

119

blowing onto the ground. But don't worry about the spillage; you will find that many species prefer to feed on the ground under the feeder. Position this type of feeder near some dense tree or shrub cover. And again, a temporary wire fence with at least 10 cm mesh will keep the cat from lunging directly under the feeder, yet will allow casual access for large birds.

Suet Feeders

You can get beef suet from the meat counter at the supermarket and birds such as woodpeckers and chickadees love it. It is a good high-energy food for birds in cold weather and is easy to maintain as it comes in a lump, lasts a while, and can be simply suspended in an old onion bag or from a string. Other types of suet feeders can be made: if you have the tools, bore holes in a short log and push suet into the holes, then hang this up.

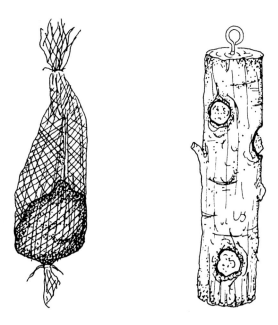

LEFT: *The simplest of all suet dispensers: an old onion bag, easily replaceable.*
RIGHT: *A more natural type of suet dispenser: an old log with holes drilled in it and stuffed with suet.*

120

Hummingbird Feeders

It is possible to attract hummingbirds into your garden with a colourful variety of flowers, but a good hummingbird feeder is one of the best ways to keep them coming back. When buying a feeder, look closely at the seals that keep the fluid in the container and choose one that looks well made. Most of them work, but the cheaper ones don't last long and frequently drip. This attracts wasps, bees and ants and leaves the feeder empty in short order. A hummingbird feeder should have some red on it, as this helps to attract the birds. You can make your own feeding fluid by dissolving two to three parts of white sugar in one to three parts of near-boiling water. Experiment and see what concentration seems to be preferred. There is no need to add red dye to the liquid, and never use honey as this ferments readily and may grow a mold that can be fatal to hummingbirds. It is important to clean the feeder frequently. In warm weather, add only a bit of liquid each time and let your feathered visitors consume it before it ferments. Keep the refill jar in the refrigerator.

Because hummingbirds are so small, it is most rewarding to hang the feeder near a window, or on the deck, where the birds quickly become accustomed to people and will allow you to watch at close range.

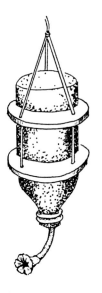

A home-made hummingbird feeder. Use an artificial red flower at the mouth.

NEST BOXES

Different species of birds have evolved to take advantage of different habitats. Each species uses a different feeding strategy and a different nesting strategy. By providing a variety of different types of food at your feeder, it is possible to attract ground-feeding birds and tree-feeding birds, seed eaters, omnivorous birds and even the odd bird of prey. The same is true if one provides a variety of different nesting opportunities. Birds will be attracted to artificial sites during the breeding season. Although some boxes may not be used the first year, they can be relocated next season.

There are many misconceptions about nest boxes. For example, birds don't need a perch on the front of the bird house — a perch is most useful for predators such as starlings that are trying to steal eggs or young. Although you may appreciate rounded corners on a bird house and a well-sanded exterior, birds prefer rough wood and a natural look. At the end of the season, clean the nest box out.

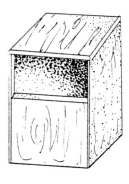

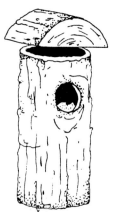

Different styles of nest boxes.

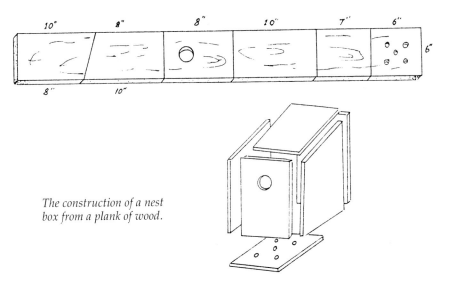

The construction of a nest box from a plank of wood.

This helps to prevent nest parasites from over-wintering, and gives birds a vacant box for the following spring. Don't disturb the house when it's in use as you may cause the adults to desert their eggs or young.

There are many different designs for nest boxes, but the most common and often the most effective is a very simple box that can be made from a single plank of wood. By altering the inside dimensions, the size of the hole, and the site where the box is placed, you should be able to attract a variety of different species.

Here are a few basic dimensions for some of the most common cavity nesting species:

Species	Floor Size	Depth	Hole Diameter	Height Above Ground
House Wren	10 x 10 cm	15 - 20 cm	2.5 cm	1 - 3 m
Black-capped Chickadee	10 x 10 cm	20 - 25 cm	3 cm	1.5 - 4.5 m
Tree Swallow	12 x 12 cm	15 - 25 cm	4 cm	1.5 - 4.5 m
Northern Flicker	20 x 20 cm	40 - 45 cm	7 cm	2.5 - 6 m

123

There are some basic rules to be kept in mind. If the nest box is exposed to full sunlight during the hottest part of the day, the nestlings may die from heat exhaustion, so choose a shaded area, or the sheltered side of an exposed tree, post or building. If the box is on a wall, the same will apply — so choose a spot that is shaded by a tree or a climbing plant. Keep the box level or tilted slightly down so that the hole is not exposed to rain. Avoid trees that cats like to climb, or put on an anti-cat barrier at the bottom: an inverted wire cone fixed to the tree about one metre above the ground usually suffices. There is nothing more upsetting than having the family cat bring you a present of the young birds that you have been watching.

Try to put the nest box in a position that looks as natural as possible and emulates a natural cavity. For your own pleasure, situate it where you can see what is going on from some convenient vantage point.

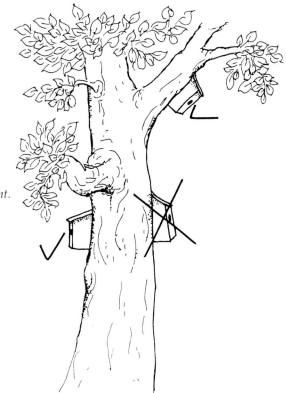

Nest box placement.

A BIRD GARDEN

Food, shelter and water are the necessities for all birds at all seasons. A simple bird feeder will bring a variety of seed-eating birds to the garden, but there is little chance of luring insect-eating birds without an appealing environment for them. Even some of the seed-eating species are very shy at the feeder and to attract these birds it is necessary to "think natural" and create some attractive mini-habitats.

It is possible to determine the types of birds that will come to your garden by providing the sort of surroundings that give them shelter, nesting opportunities and food. Flycatchers and other insect-eating birds will be attracted in spring and summer to flower gardens where insects are likely to be abundant. Seed-eating birds will find both shelter and food in the wilder sections of a back yard, where shrubs and weeds combine to provide dense cover and year-round access to food in the form of seeds. A varied garden plot will lure birds where a flawless lawn will not, and a mix of shrubs and taller trees will attract a far greater variety and abundance of birds than a hedge of uniform trees or shrubs. It is not only berry bushes and fruit trees that provide food; seeds, insects feeding on plants, and water are at least as likely to entice birds.

Birds are also attracted to gardens where there is plenty of shelter in which to rest during the day, or to roost at night, where they can escape from the hottest weather in the summer, and find some protection in the winter. Gardens with mature trees and plenty of shrub cover will be attractive. Some birds also appreciate an area of longer grass and if it is possible to keep an area of the garden as "wild" as you can, it will attract all sorts of creatures, not just birds.

Planting to Attract Birds

Trees and Bushes An adequate food and cover supply are prerequisites for the attraction of wildlife. To achieve optimum habitat for your property, trees, shrubs and plants of diverse characteristics should be planted. Tall trees, such as most oaks or maples, provide an upper storey canopy for birds like Red-eyed Vireos and Northern Orioles. The existence of this habitat is most often limited to long-established districts within a city, or large semi-rural estate lots. It may not be practical for the average subdivision home owner to consider planting these species because the average lot is too small to accommodate them.

Sapsucker drilling holes.

On the other hand, diversified habitat may be achieved by the selection of plantings that will provide ground cover or low shrubbery for species that prefer habitat either close to or on the ground. Song Sparrows and Rufous-sided Towhees are examples.

Shrubs and trees of medium height will attract still other species. The more habitat variety you can provide, the greater are your chances of attracting a variety of birds.

As with habitat, distinct preferences are exhibited by birds in their food requirements. Some species prefer soft berries while others are attracted to flower seeds or to seeds from conifer cones. Many other species are insectivorous and feed on the insects that abound on the shrubbery or the bark of trees. Young nestlings of all species are fed the soft insect larvae that are found about the leaves.

Evergreens are indispensable in a properly balanced planting program because they provide shelter and food, and interesting dark background for shrubs and flowers. On large lots they can be planted in clumps of three to five trees, two metres apart, or in double rows to form wildlife travel lanes along the edge of the property. A single evergreen planted on a small lot and surrounded by shrubs can provide some protection. Suitable species include white cedar, white spruce, and if your lot is large enough, eastern hemlock and white pine.

In addition to conifers, seed-eating birds find alders and birches attractive. The cones provide an abundance of seed that is eagerly sought by such winter birds as Common Redpolls and Pine Siskins.

The winged seeds of the Manitoba maple are particular favourites of Evening Grosbeaks. This tree is exceptionally fast growing and can provide food, shade and cover in a relatively short period of time. The rapid growth can be a disadvantage, however, to the small lot owner, as the tree can soon crowd out other desirable species.

Acorns rate close to the top of any wildlife food list because they are a staple in the diet of a large number of wildlife species, particularly during the critical winter season. Blue Jays, woodpeckers and squirrels are especially partial to oak trees.

The European mountain ash is a highly attractive ornamental tree. The ripe fruit is avidly eaten by Robins, Cedar Waxwings and other birds. Should the fruit not be eaten in the fall, it will persist throughout the winter, adding a touch of bright colour to the yard and providing a ready food supply for groups of wandering songbirds like waxwings.

Native hawthorns should not be overlooked in any backyard planting, for they possess colourful blossoms in the spring and

Starling resting on a fence post.

127

fruit that can persist throughout the winter. The protective thorns make the tree excellent cover for shelter and breeding.

Autumn olive is a versatile shrub that can reach as high as five metres when fully grown. It offers suitable nesting habitat for many songbirds, and as a plant barrier attracts rabbits and pheasants to the shelter of its spreading branches. The berries ripen in clusters and persist on the branches throughout the winter.

The native viburnums, dogwoods and honeysuckles are useful shrubs because they provide a desirable landscape effect and adequate sites for shelter, nesting, and a reliable food supply. The native high-bush cranberry has brilliant scarlet-coloured autumn foliage and bright red berries that cling to the branches over winter. Although normally unpalatable to birds, the berries provide an emergency food supply. Nannyberry, one of the taller viburnums, reaches a height of between seven and nine metres. Persisting until late fall and early winter, the blue-black fruit is attractive to the Brown Thrasher as well as other species.

Fruits of most native dogwoods ripen in late summer or early fall, so provide little in the way of winter food. The woody branches of the red-osier dogwood, however, present a pleasing contrast against the winter snow.

Honeysuckles are often grown for their flowers and are attractive to Ruby-throated Hummingbirds. Elderberries provide an important food source, as the dark, mature fruit is ravenously eaten by most songbirds, including thrushes and warblers. Once discovered, the fruit is eaten within a few days.

The dense foliage of wild grape offers unusually good cover for small birds. The fruit is a favourite food of many songbirds, especially Northern Flickers and Northern Cardinals, and the bark is often used in nest construction. Planted along a sunny fence, grapevines make a good visual barrier.

Ground-feeding birds such a Dark-eyed Juncos and White-throated Sparrows benefit from the provision of ample ground cover. The low, spreading evergreen junipers provide excellent cover and can be planted along the edge of the patio or at the base of specimen trees.

Flowers Patches of carefully selected flowers will provide continuous colour in the garden as well as being an important food source for birds. Some common plants that produce an abundance of seed include sunflowers, cosmos, zinnias and asters. American Goldfinches seem to be particularly fond of cosmos seed. If the seed heads are left to stand throughout the winter, Dark-eyed Juncos, Blue Jays and others could well be attracted.

A specialized flower garden can be planted to attract Ruby-throated Hummingbirds. These birds readily visit morning glories, honeysuckles, hollyhocks, and columbines.

Water Birds need water throughout the year. A bird bath that is kept unfrozen in the coldest weather will attract many birds. During the summer months, a bird bath can become a busy place. Birds like to bathe more in the summer, and bird baths can provide endless pleasure for both the birds and the birdwatcher.

Choose or build a bird bath that is not too deep (no more than 7 cm), shelves gradually and is finished in a rough texture so that it is easy for birds to grip. Birds get engrossed in drinking and bathing and when they have wet feathers, they don't fly quite so well. Therefore, if the bath is on or near ground level, make sure that it is situated well away from bushes, so that cats cannot approach the bath unseen.

You can keep the water in your bird bath unfrozen during the coldest winters with a small heater available on the market, and you can make the bath particularly attractive to birds in summer by creating a trickly flow or spray of water with a small electric pump.

SEASONS OF BIRDWATCHING

Spring

The first sign of spring is often the increase in the number of ducks on the rivers and lakes as birds from the south push north, waiting for the break-up of the ice on their inland breeding sites. One of the first ducks to arrive may be the elegant Northern Pintail. Also arriving in early spring are Tree Swallows, Red-winged Blackbirds and Song Sparrows.

This is the time of the year when bird-song also begins and many birds that have overwintered suddenly become more noticeable as they begin to establish breeding territories. Some species, such as the Great Horned Owl, which is here throughout the year, is best found at this time of the year. Take a walk through one of the forested parks around the city at dusk or before dawn and you may well be rewarded by hearing it.

The increase in bird activity is the prelude to the breeding season and you will notice that many of the birds are actively involved in courtship behaviour. Waterfowl go through many of their breeding displays on the water, and some are very attractive to watch, particularly those of the goldeneyes and Bufflehead.

Like the Mallard, the Bufflehead's courtship is far from sedate, with the female frequently being pursued none too gallantly by many males.

Spring is also the time of year when it is easiest to see birds in and around the city. Not only are the numbers and variety of birds swelled by the migrants that are arriving to breed, or passing through on their way to northern breeding grounds, but the lack of leaves on the deciduous trees makes seeing them much easier. Without doubt, early May is the best time to watch for warblers. Your backyard or local park may be alive with brightly coloured birds one morning but quiet the next, as the birds continue their migratory journey. Later in the year, not only will it be harder to spot them, but the young "look-alike" birds will confuse even the most experienced birder.

The display of a male Red-winged Blackbird during the mating season.

Summer

Late spring and summer is the breeding season for most birds and this means a great deal of singing. Once the serious business of incubating the eggs and feeding the young starts, birds become less noticeable and once more secretive. It can be an advantage for a bird to announce its presence when trying to attract a mate or establish a territory, but once eggs are laid and the young hatch, there is a greater need to incubate and feed young birds, and to remain undetected by predators.

For those who have put up nest boxes or have the good fortune to have their trees or gardens selected as nesting sites, this time can be great fun. There is something enormously satisfying about witnessing the breeding cycle of birds. From start to finish, it may take a chickadee only about a month to find a mate, build a nest, lay eggs, hatch them and feed the young to the point of fledging. If they happen to use a nest box that you have put up for them, this becomes a very personal experience and the sense of thrill when the young birds fly comes as quite a surprise.

Ducks moult at this time of year and both the males and the females look very much alike for a while. When ducks are moulting, it is known as the "eclipse" plumage; some species can look very different and even the common male Mallard may require more than one look before identification is possible. Birds moult at this time of year to renew their flight feathers before their fall migration, while there is still an abundance of summer food available.

Autumn

As early as August, birds that have completed their breeding cycle for the year will begin to start their migration south. Birds that breed in the Arctic must complete their breeding as quickly as possible because, by late summer, food sources are already less abundant and colder weather has begun. As young birds fledge, the birds leave their breeding grounds and begin to arrive. Watch for the increase in numbers f shorebirds and waterfowl now.

Rivers, bays and lakes with muddy shores, and marshes are particularly good places to visit at this time of year.

Autumn is also the time of year when warblers and many of the other small birds can be frustratingly hard to identify, as the young birds and the moulting adults do not always look the way they ought to according to the books!

Swallows begin to flock in huge, noticeable numbers, but by Labour Day, many have departed. We become aware that our common summer residents are more difficult to find but the migrants from the north attract our attention.

Autumn is the best time to watch out for rarer birds, so be prepared to take a close look at anything that seems odd or unusual. Migrants, especially juveniles, can easily take the wrong turn. Check every bird in a flock of ducks or shorebirds and look for colours or features that are different from the majority's. Then check your field guide to see if you have found a rarity. If you think you have, call the museum.

Winter

Here in the Ottawa valley, we can look forward to seeing some bird species not readily found here at other times of the year. Waterfowl on the river during the winter can be a source of many hours of enjoyable bird watching. Scour the fast moving water for goldeneyes and mergansers.

Early winter is the time of year when feeders work particularly well in attracting birds into the garden. Once you have attracted a few, more will show up and linger on — perhaps even through the winter — because there is safety in numbers. Many birds react swiftly to the danger signals of other species. Although most of the smaller birds will have migrated south, some of the woodland species can be easier to see at this time of year, as there are fewer leaves on the deciduous trees and bushes. Look out for Downy and Hairy Woodpeckers, which always seem more visible in the winter, as well as winter visitors like Evening and Pine Grosbeaks and Bohemian Waxwings.

Winter is always an interesting season to birdwatch. You never know what to expect, a Snowy Owl, Gyrfalcon or a covey of Hungarian Partridge.

KEEPING BIRD NOTES

Now that you have birds coming to the feeder and birds nesting in the bird boxes, why not keep a record of which birds you see in your yard, how many of them there are, and how often you see them? Keeping records is the only way of noting changes and will provide you with many hours of pleasure. A daily or weekly checklist of sightings will tell you a great deal about your avian visitors. It will furnish a record of how numbers change throughout the seasons and from year to year, and of specific migration times of many species. You will soon know just when to expect your first Ruby-throated Hummingbird of the spring, or the first Dark-eyed Junco of the autumn. The FON's bird checklist, which you can find at the back of this book, may be especially helpful to you. It shows the geographic distribution of many Ontarian birds, their breeding status, and their relative occurrence; if you spot a

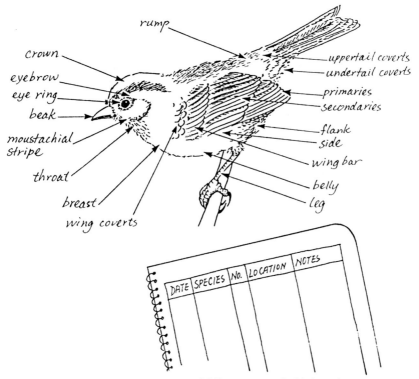

It is important to know the names of different parts of a bird, so that you can jot down specific information in your bird log.

bird which is uncommon to your area, or out of its normal range (extralimital), it would be a good idea to record it and report it to the FON. You can get additional copies of this checklist from the FON at minimal cost.

If you spend time hiking through nearby natural areas or parks, your observations will help you to remember what you saw and when. These observations will tell you what birds were common in which years and what parts of the area were particularly good for various species. As well as being of interest to you, you may be able to make an important contribution to local knowledge by helping ornithologists understand how numbers of birds in your area are changing. This sort of information is often not available when it is needed, and may also help to protect your favorite birding spot, should it be threatened with development. You could even take part in one of the many Christmas Bird Counts held in the province during the holidays; similar counts are taken of wintering birds all over North America. (You can get a list of coordinators' names from the FON.)

Keeping good records may allow you to convince the experts that you have seen a particularly rare bird, or may help you describe a problem species to an expert. Try to record a clear image of what the bird looked like — a simple line sketch is fine, although a photograph of the bird is often required for confirmation of a sighting. Include as much information as you can about the bird, its plumage characteristics, its bill, leg colour, sounds, and what behaviour the bird exhibited.

You might also want to keep a bird log. This would include the species you saw, how many, where and when (see diagram).

Keep your records in a notebook to avoid losing them. If you intend to take your notebook on hikes, choose one that has a soft waterproof cover; this will allow you to stuff it into a pocket or your pack and it will not disintegrate in the rain. A useful tip: pencils are easier than pens to sketch with, and they write more easily on damp paper.

Another good way to learn more about birds is to join your local natural history or bird society. You will meet many knowledgeable people who will be pleased to teach you what they know about birds and the best places to see them in various areas. Many organizations run field trips to some of the good birdwatching spots and provide the benefit of an expert to help with identification problems.

Good birding!

FEDERATION OF ONTARIO NATURALISTS AND ONTARIO FIELD ORNITHOLOGISTS

Field Checklist of Birds

(1988)

This list comprises all of the bird species (437) which have been recorded in the Province of Ontario, on the basis of specimens, photographs, recordings or documented sight records accepted by the Ontario Bird Records Committee (OBRC).

The list appeared with scientific names in Ontario Birds V2, No. 1 (1984). Classification and Nomenclature follow the A.O.U. Check-List of North American Birds (6th ed. 1984), and its Supplements.

LOCALITY			
TIME/DATE			
MONTH			
YEAR			
OBSERVER			

LEGEND

Ontario is divided into north and south regions at approximately 47°N.

N - Species recorded in North; [N] indicates the OBRC requests documentation when the species is recorded in the region.

S - Species recorded in South; [S] indicates the OBRC requests documentation when the species is recorded in the region.

* - Breeding species

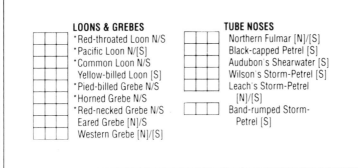

LOONS & GREBES
*Red-throated Loon N/S
*Pacific Loon N/[S]
*Common Loon N/S
Yellow-billed Loon [S]
*Pied-billed Grebe N/S
*Horned Grebe N/S
*Red-necked Grebe N/S
Eared Grebe [N]/S
Western Grebe [N]/[S]

TUBE NOSES
Northern Fulmar [N]/[S]
Black-capped Petrel [S]
Audubon's Shearwater [S]
Wilson's Storm-Petrel [S]
Leach's Storm-Petrel [N]/[S]
Band-rumped Storm-Petrel [S]

GANNETS, PELICANS & CORMORANTS

- Northern Gannet [N]/[S]
- *American White Pelican N/[S]
- Brown Pelican [S]
- Great Cormorant [S]
- *Double-crested Cormorant N/S
- Anhinga [S]

HERONS, STORKS & IBISES

- *American Bittern N/S
- *Least Bittern [N]/S
- *Great Blue Heron N/S
- *Great Egret [N]/S
- *Snowy Egret [N]/S
- Little Blue Heron [N]/[S]
- Tricolored Heron [N]/[S]
- *Cattle Egret [N]/S
- *Green-backed Heron [N]/S
- *Black-crowned Night-Heron [N]/S
- Yellow-crowned Night-Heron [S]
- White Ibis [S]
- Glossy Ibis [S]
- Wood Stork [S]

SWANS, GEESE & DUCKS

- Fulvous Whistling-Duck [S]
- *Tundra Swan [S]
- Trumpeter Swan [S]
- • Mute Swan [N]/S
- Greater White-fronted Goose N/[S]
- *Snow Goose N/S
- *Ross' Goose N
- Brant N/S
- *Canada Goose N/S
- *Wood Duck N/S
- *Green-winged Teal N/S
- *American Black Duck N/S
- *Mallard N/S
- *Northern Pintail N/S
- *Blue-winged Teal N/S
- *Cinnamon Teal [N]/[S]
- *Northern Shoveler N/S

- *Gadwall N/S
- Eurasian Wigeon [N]/[S]
- *American Wigeon N/S
- *Canvasback N/S
- *Redhead N/S
- *Ring-necked Duck N/S
- Tufted Duck [S]
- *Greater Scaup N/S
- *Lesser Scaup N/S
- *Common Eider N/[S]
- *King Eider N/S
- Harlequin Duck [N]/S
- *Oldsquaw N/S
- Black Scoter N/S
- *Surf Scoter N/S
- *White-winged Scoter N/S
- *Common Goldeneye N/S
- Barrow's Goldeneye [N]/S
- *Bufflehead N/S
- Smew [S]
- *Hooded Merganser N/S
- *Common Merganser N/S
- *Red-breasted Merganser N/S
- *Ruddy Duck N/S

VULTURES, HAWKS, EAGLES & FALCONS

- Black Vulture [S]
- *Turkey Vulture N/S
- *Osprey N/S
- American Swallow-tailed Kite [N]/[S]
- Mississippi Kite [S]
- *Bald Eagle N/S
- *Northern Harrier N/S
- *Sharp-shinned Hawk N/S
- *Cooper's Hawk N/S
- *Northern Goshawk N/S
- *Red-shouldered Hawk N/S
- *Broad-winged Hawk N/S
- Swainson's Hawk [N]/[S]
- *Red-tailed Hawk N/S
- *Rough-legged Hawk N/S
- *Golden Eagle N/S
- Crested Caracara [N]
- • American Kestrel N/S
- *Merlin N/S
- *Peregrine Falcon N/S
- Gyrfalcon N/[S]

GROUSE & TURKEYS
* Gray Partridge N/S
* Ring-necked Pheasant N/S
* Spruce Grouse N/S
* Willow Ptarmigan N/[S]
  Rock Ptarmigan N
* Ruffed Grouse N/S
* Greater Prairie-Chicken [N]/[S]
* Sharp-tailed Grouse N/S
* Wild Turkey S
* Northern Bobwhite S

RAILS & CRANES
* Yellow Rail N/S
* King Rail S
* Virginia Rail N/S
* Sora N/S
  Purple Gallinule [N]/[S]
* Common Moorhen [N]/S
* American Coot N/S
* Sandhill Crane N/S
  Whooping Crane [S]

SHOREBIRDS
  Black-bellied Plover N/S
* Lesser Golden-Plover N/S
  Mongolian Plover [S]
  Snowy Plover [S]
* Semipalmated Plover N/S
* Piping Plover N/[S]
* Killdeer N/S
  American Oystercatcher [S]
  Black-necked Stilt [N]/[S]
* American Avocet [N]/[S]
* Greater Yellowlegs N/S
* Lesser Yellowlegs N/S
  Spotted Redshank [S]
* Solitary Sandpiper N/S
  Willet [N]/S
  Wandering Tattler [S]
* Spotted Sandpiper N/S
* Upland Sandpiper N/S
  Eskimo Curlew [N]/[S]
* Whimbrel N/S
  Slender-billed Curlew [S]
  Long-billed Curlew [S]
* Hudsonian Godwit N/S
* Marbled Godwit N/S
  Ruddy Turnstone N/S
  Red Knot N/S
  Sanderling N/S
* Semipalmated Sandpiper N/S
  Western Sandpiper [N]/S
  Little Stint [N]
* Least Sandpiper N/S
  White-rumped Sandpiper N/S
  Baird s Sandpiper N/S
* Pectoral Sandpiper N/S
  Sharp-tailed Sandpiper [S]
  Purple Sandpiper N/S
* Dunlin N/S
  Curlew Sandpiper [N]/[S]
* Stilt Sandpiper N/S
  Buff-breasted Sandpiper N/S
  Ruff [N]/S
* Short-billed Dowitcher N/S
  Long-billed Dowitcher [N]/S
* Common Snipe N/S
* American Woodcock N/S
* Wilson s Phalarope N/S
* Red-necked Phalarope N/S
  Red Phalarope N/S

JAEGERS, GULLS, TERNS & SKIMMERS
  Pomarine Jaeger [N]/[S]
* Parasitic Jaeger N/S
  Long-tailed Jaeger N/[S]
  Laughing Gull [N]/S
  Franklin s Gull N/S
* Little Gull N/S
  Common Black-headed Gull [N]/S
* Bonaparte s Gull N/S
  Mew Gull [S]
* Ring-billed Gull N/S
* California Gull [S]
* Herring Gull N/S
  Thayer s Gull N/S
  Iceland Gull N/S
  Lesser Black-backed Gull [N]/S
  Glaucous Gull N/S
* Great Black-backed Gull N/S

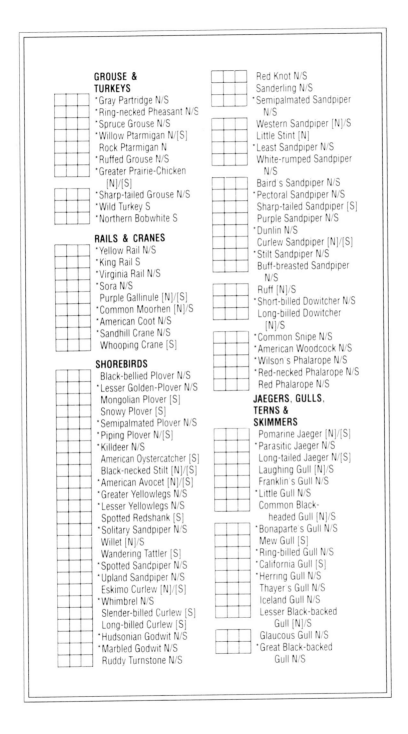

137

Black-legged
   Kittiwake [N]/S
Ross' Gull [N]
Sabine's Gull N/S
Ivory Gull [N]/[S]
*Caspian Tern N/S
Royal Tern [S]
Sandwich Tern [S]
*Common Tern N/S
*Arctic Tern N/S
*Forster's Tern N/S
Least Tern [S]
Sooty Tern [S]
*Black Tern N/S
Black Skimmer [N]/[S]

ALCIDS
Dovekie [S]
Thick-billed Murre [S]
Razorbill [S]
*Black Guillemot N/[S]
Ancient Murrelet [S]
Atlantic Puffin [S]

PIGEONS & DOVES
*Rock Dove N/S
Band-tailed Pigeon [N]/[S]
White-winged Dove [N]/[S]
*Mourning Dove N/S
*Passenger Pigeon-Extinct
Common Ground Dove [N]

CUCKOOS & ANIS
*Black-billed Cuckoo N/S
*Yellow-billed Cuckoo N/S
Groove-billed Ani [N]/[S]

OWLS
*Common Barn-Owl [N]/S
*Eastern Screech-Owl [N]/S
*Great Horned Owl N/S
Snowy Owl N/S
*Northern Hawk-Owl N/S
Burrowing Owl [N]/[S]
*Barred Owl N/S
*Great Gray Owl N/S
*Long-eared Owl N/S
*Short-eared Owl N/S
*Boreal Owl N/S
*Northern Saw-whet Owl
   N/S

GOATSUCKERS
Lesser Nighthawk [S]
*Common Nighthawk N/S
Common Poorwill [N]
*Chuck-will's-widow S
*Whip-poor-will N/S

SWIFTS & HUMMINGBIRDS
*Chimney Swift N/S
*Ruby-throated
   Hummingbird N/S
Rufous Hummingbird
   [N]/[S]

KINGFISHERS
*Belted Kingfisher N/S

WOODPECKERS
Lewis' Woodpecker [S]
*Red-headed
   Woodpecker N/S
*Red-bellied
   Woodpecker [N]/S
*Yellow-bellied
   Sapsucker N/S
*Downy Woodpecker N/S
*Hairy Woodpecker N/S
*Three-toed
   Woodpecker N/S
*Black-backed
   Woodpecker N/S
*Northern Flicker N/S
*Pileated
   Woodpecker N/S

TYRANT FLYCATCHERS
*Olive-sided
   Flycatcher N/S
Western
   Wood-Pewee [N]
*Eastern
   Wood-Pewee N/S
*Yellow-bellied
   Flycatcher N/S
*Acadian Flycatcher S
*Alder Flycatcher N/S
*Willow Flycatcher [N]/S
*Least Flycatcher N/S
Gray Flycatcher [S]

☐ •Eastern Phoebe N/S
☐ Say's Phoebe [N]/[S]
☐ Vermilion
Flycatcher [S]
☐ Ash-throated
Flycatcher [S]
☐ •Great Crested
Flycatcher N/S
☐ Sulphur-bellied
Flycatcher [S]
☐ Cassin's Kingbird [S]
☐ •Western Kingbird [N]/[S]
☐ •Eastern Kingbird N/S
☐ Gray Kingbird [S]
☐ Scissor-tailed Flycatcher
[N]/[S]
☐ Fork-tailed Flycatcher [N]

LARKS, MARTINS & SWALLOWS
☐ •Horned Lark N/S
☐ •Purple Martin N/S
☐ •Tree Swallow N/S
☐ •Northern Rough-
winged Swallow N/S
☐ •Bank Swallow N/S
☐ •Cliff Swallow N/S
☐ •Barn Swallow N/S

JAYS, MAGPIES & CROWS
☐ •Gray Jay N/S
☐ •Blue Jay N/S
☐ Clark's Nutcracker [N]
☐ •Black-billed Magpie N/[S]
☐ Eurasian Jackdaw [S]
☐ •American Crow N/S
☐ Fish Crow [S]
☐ •Common Raven N/S

TITMICE, NUTHATCHES & CREEPERS
☐ •Black-capped
Chickadee N/S
☐ Carolina Chickadee [S]
☐ •Boreal Chickadee N/S
☐ •Tufted Titmouse S
☐ •Red-breasted
Nuthatch N/S
☐ •White-breasted
Nuthatch N/S
☐ •Brown Creeper N/S

WRENS
☐ Rock Wren [N]/[S]
☐ •Carolina Wren S
☐ •Bewick's Wren [S]
☐ •House Wren N/S
☐ •Winter Wren N/S
☐ •Sedge Wren N/S
☐ •Marsh Wren N/S

KINGLETS, GNATCATCHERS, THRUSHES & MIMIDS
☐ •Golden-crowned
Kinglet N/S
☐ •Ruby-crowned
Kinglet N/S
☐ •Blue-gray
Gnatcatcher [N]/S
☐ Siberian Rubythroat [S]
☐ Northern Wheatear [N]/[S]
☐ •Eastern Bluebird N/S
☐ Mountain Bluebird [N]/[S]
☐ Townsend's Solitaire
[N]/[S]
☐ •Veery N/S
☐ •Gray-cheeked
Thrush N/S
☐ •Swainson's Thrush N/S
☐ •Hermit Thrush N/S
☐ •Wood Thrush N/S
☐ Eurasian Blackbird [S]
☐ Fieldfare [S]
☐ •American Robin N/S
☐ Varied Thrush [N]/[S]
☐ •Gray Catbird N/S
☐ •Northern
Mockingbird N/S
☐ Sage Thrasher [N]/[S]
☐ •Brown Thrasher N/S

PIPITS, WAXWINGS, SHRIKES & STARLINGS
☐ •Water Pipit N/S
☐ Sprague's Pipit [N]
☐ Bohemian Waxwing N/S
☐ •Cedar Waxwing N/S
☐ Phainopepla [S]
☐ •Northern Shrike N/S

* Loggerhead Shrike [N]/S
* European Starling N/S

VIREOS
* White-eyed Vireo [N]/S
  Bell's Vireo [S]
* Solitary Vireo N/S
* Yellow-throated
  Vireo N/S
* Warbling Vireo N/S
* Philadelphia Vireo N/S
* Red-eyed Vireo N/S

WOOD WARBLERS
* Blue-winged
  Warbler [N]/S
* Golden-winged
  Warbler N/S
* Tennessee Warbler N/S
* Orange-crowned
  Warbler N/S
* Nashville Warbler N/S
  Virginia's Warbler [S]
* Northern Parula N/S
* Yellow Warbler N/S
* Chestnut-sided
  Warbler N/S
* Magnolia Warbler N/S
* Cape May Warbler N/S
* Black-throated
  Blue Warbler N/S
* Yellow-rumped
  Warbler N/S
  Black-throated
  Gray Warbler [S]
  Townsend's Warbler [S]
  Hermit Warbler [S]
* Black-throated
  Green Warbler N/S
* Blackburnian
  Warbler N/S
  Yellow-throated
  Warbler [N]/[S]
* Pine Warbler N/S
* Kirtland's Warbler [S]
* Prairie Warbler S
* Palm Warbler N/S
* Bay-breasted
  Warbler N/S
* Blackpoll Warbler N/S

* Cerulean Warbler S
* Black-and-white
  Warbler N/S
* American Redstart N/S
* Prothonotary
  Warbler [N]/S
  Worm-eating
  Warbler S
  Swainson's Warbler [S]
* Ovenbird N/S
* Northern
  Waterthrush N/S
* Louisiana
  Waterthrush S
  Kentucky Warbler S
* Connecticut
  Warbler N/S
* Mourning Warbler N/S
  MacGillivray's
  Warbler [S]
* Common
  Yellowthroat N/S
* Hooded Warbler [N]/S
* Wilson's Warbler N/S
* Canada Warbler N/S
  Painted Redstart [S]
* Yellow-breasted
  Chat [N]/S

TANAGERS
  Summer Tanager [N]/S
* Scarlet Tanager N/S
  Western Tanager [N]/[S]

GROSBEAKS, BUNTINGS & SPARROWS
* Northern Cardinal [N]/S
* Rose-breasted
  Grosbeak N/S
  Black-headed
  Grosbeak [N]/[S]
  Blue Grosbeak [S]
  Lazuli Bunting [N]/[S]
* Indigo Bunting N/S
* Dickcissel [N]/S
  Green-tailed
  Towhee [S]
* Rufous-sided
  Towhee [N]/S
  Bachman's Sparrow [S]

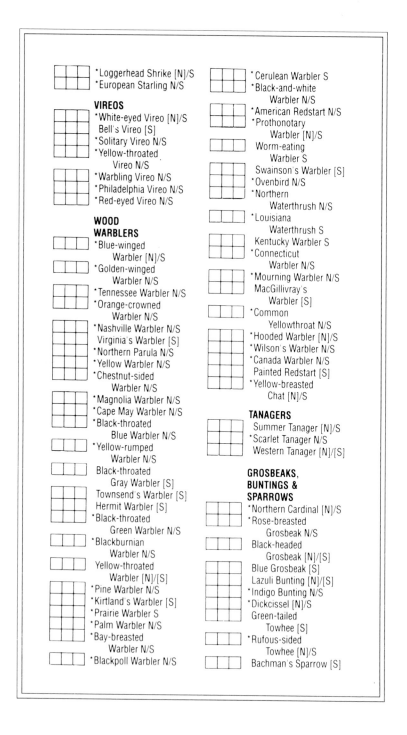

Cassin's Sparrow [N]/[S]
*American Tree
    Sparrow N/S
*Chipping Sparrow N/S
*Clay-colored
    Sparrow N/S
*Field Sparrow [N]/S
*Vesper Sparrow N/S
*Lark Sparrow [N]/[S]
Lark Bunting [N]/[S]
*Savannah Sparrow N/S
*Grasshopper
    Sparrow [N]/S
*Henslow's Sparrow S
*Le Conte's Sparrow N/S
*Sharp-tailed
    Sparrow N/S
*Fox Sparrow N/S
*Song Sparrow N/S
*Lincoln's Sparrow N/S
*Swamp Sparrow N/S
*White-throated
    Sparrow N/S
Golden-crowned
    Sparrow [N]/[S]
*White-crowned
    Sparrow N/S
*Harris' Sparrow N/[S]
*Dark-eyed Junco N/S
*Lapland Longspur N/S
*Smith's Longspur N/[S]
Chestnut-collared
    Longspur [N]/[S]
Snow Bunting N/S

MEADOWLARKS, BLACKBIRDS & ORIOLES

*Bobolink N/S
*Red-winged
    Blackbird N/S
*Eastern Meadowlark N/S
*Western
    Meadowlark N/S
*Yellow-headed
    Blackbird N/S
*Rusty Blackbird N/S
*Brewer's Blackbird N/S
Great-tailed Grackle [N]
*Common Grackle N/S

*Brown-headed
    Cowbird N/S
*Orchard Oriole [N]/S
*Northern Oriole N/S
Scott's Oriole [N]

FINCHES

Brambling [N]
Rosy Finch [N]
*Pine Grosbeak N/S
*Purple Finch N/S
*House Finch [N]/S
*Red Crossbill N/S
*White-winged
    Crossbill N/S
*Common Redpoll N/S
Hoary Redpoll N/S
*Pine Siskin N/S
Lesser Goldfinch [S]
*American Goldfinch N/S
*Evening Grosbeak N/S

WEAVER FINCHES

*House Sparrow N/S

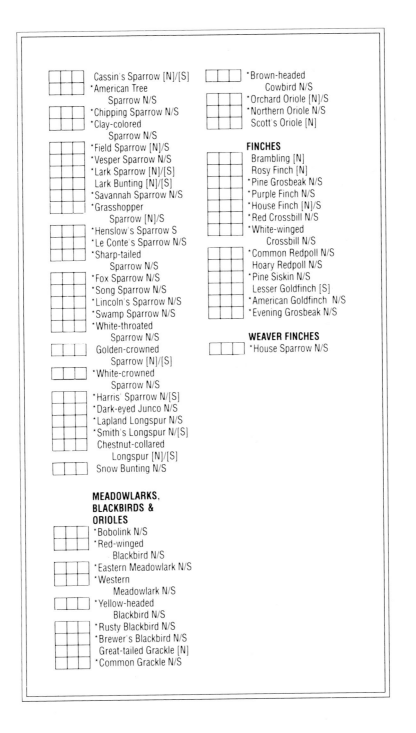

141

SUGGESTED READING

Brunton, Daniel F. 1988. *Nature and Natural Areas in Canada's Capital*. Ottawa Citizen and the Ottawa Field Naturalists' Club, Ottawa

Cadman, M.D., P. Eagles and F. Heilleiner. 1987. *Atlas of the Breeding Birds of Ontario*. University of Waterloo Press, Waterloo, Ontario.

Godfrey, W.E. 1986. *The Birds of Canada (Second Edition)*. National Museum of Natural Sciences, Ottawa, Ontario.

Goodwin, C.E. 1982. *A Bird Finding Guide to Ontario*. University of Toronto Press.

Kress, S.W. 1985. *The Audubon Society Guide to Attracting Birds*. Charles Scribner's Sons. New York.

McElroy, T.P. 1974. *The Habitat Guide to Birding*. Alfred A. Knopf, Inc., New York.

OFNC, 1985. *A Birder's Checklist of Ottawa*. Ottawa Field Naturalists' Club, Ottawa

OFNC, 1967. Ongoing. *Trail and Landscape*. The Ottawa Field Naturalists' Club, Ottawa. Quarterly Publication

Sankey, John 1987. *Enjoying the Birds of the Ottawa Valley*. Range Press Ottawa

Terres, J.K. 1982. *The Audubon Society Encyclopedia of North American Birds*. Alfred A. Knopf, New York, N.Y.

DIRECTORY OF ORGANIZATIONS

Canadian Nature Federation
453 Sussex Drive
Ottawa, Ontario
K1N 9Z9

Federation of Ontario Naturalists
355 Lesmill Road
Don Mills, Ontario
M3B 2W8
Telephone: 444-8419

*Le Club des Ornithologues
de l'Outaouais*
Box 419
Station A
Hull, Quebec
J8Y 6P2

Ottawa Field Naturalists' Club
Box 3264
Station C
Ottawa, Ontario
K1Y 4J5

Pembroke and Area Bird Club
Box 1242
Pembroke, Ontario
K8A 6Y6

Rideau Trail Association
Box 15
Kingston, Ontario
K7L 4V6

INDEX TO BIRDS

ABOUT THE AUTHOR

Gerald McKeating has spent many years birding in Southern Ontario. Long active in conservation issues, he spent five years as executive director of the Federation of Ontario Naturalists before moving to the Ontario Ministry of Resources where he was responsible for the nongame and endangered species programs.

Since 1979, Gerry has worked with the Canadian Wildlife Service where he is now head of habitat conservation for the Western and Northern Region in Edmonton, Alberta.

ABOUT THE ILLUSTRATORS

Lead illustrator Ewa Pluciennik, who specialize in water colour and oil painting, was born and raise in Opole, Silesia, Poland where she receive her artistic training. She has been living in Canada for nearly five years.

Contributing illustrators Kitty Ho and Donna McKinnon are freelance artists living in Alberta. Johnston lives in British Columbia.